YESHIVA GEDOLAH
BAIS YISROEL

2002 Avenue J • Brooklyn, NY 11210 • (718) 258-7400

Over the last decade, New York City has witnessed the growth of Yeshiva Gedolah Bais Yisroel, one of the most promising new institutions of Torah scholarship. Built on the traditions of the great *yeshivos* that once flourished in Europe, producing generations of Torah leaders and *talmidei chachamim*, Yeshiva Gedolah Bais Yisroel attracts many outstanding students through the high standard of excellence of its learning program and the atmosphere of warmth and personal attention that pervade the halls of the *yeshivah*.

Yeshiva Gedolah Bais Yisroel is guided by its world-renowned *menahel ruchani* and mentor HaRav Avigdor Miller, *shlita*. HaRav Miller is known as a *Baal Mussar* who has had a great impact on our generation. His *shmuezzen* and shining example has a profound effect on our *talmidim*.

The *rosh yeshivah* and founder of Yeshiva Gedolah Bais Yisroel is HaRav Shmuel Miller, *shlita*, one of the leading *talmidim* of HaRav Aharon Kotler, *zt"l*, and HaRav Yosef Ber Soloveitchik, *zt"l*. He is known as a gifted *marbitz Torah* whose lucid *shiurim* have successfully molded hundreds of *talmidim*. The students are drawn to his warmth and sensitivity.

The *talmidim* of Yeshiva Gedolah Bais Yisroel thrive on their curriculum, a blend of *lomdus* and *mussar* absorbed by the founders of the *yeshivah* from their *rebbeim*. Spurred on by its success, Yeshiva Gedolah Bais Yisroel was expanded to include a *mesivta* high school which combines the system of *lomdus* and *mussar* together with guidance in *middos* and *yiras shomayim*. The *mesivta* is led by Rabbi Mordechai Mandelbaum, the principal, aided by an exceptional staff of *rebbeim*, and its high-quality secular studies program is taught by fully-trained and licensed teachers. In just a short time, many of the products of Yeshiva Gedolah Bais Yisrael have become successful teachers and Torah leaders filling important positions in the broader Torah community.

Yeshiva Gedolah Bais Yisroel continues to grow and has recently moved to a newly built edifice in a thriving neighborhood in the Flatbush section of Brooklyn. The presence of the *yeshivah* is sure to have an uplifting effect on the whole neighborhood. The future of Yeshiva Gedolah Bais Yisroel is full of opportunities as it takes its place amongst the most promising Torah institutions of our time.

הסטוריה

The ArtScroll History Series®

Rabbi Nosson Scherman / Rabbi Meir Zlotowitz

General Editors

PILLAR

by
Menachem Mendel

translated by
Shaindel Weinbach

OF FIRE

EPISODES IN THE LIFE OF THE BRISKER RAV, RABBI YEHOSHUA LEIB DISKIN

Published by

Mesorah Publications, ltd

FIRST EDITION
First Impression . . . July, 1992

Special Edition for
Yeshiva Gedolah Bais Yisroel
August, 1992

Published and Distributed by
MESORAH PUBLICATIONS, Ltd.
Brooklyn, New York 11232

Distributed in Israel by
MESORAH MAFITZIM / J. GROSSMAN
Rechov Harav Uziel 117
Jerusalem, Israel

Distributed in Australia & New Zealand by
GOLD'S BOOK & GIFT CO.
36 William Street
Balaclava 3183, Vic., Australia

Distributed in Europe by
J. LEHMANN HEBREW BOOKSELLERS
20 Cambridge Terrace
Gateshead, Tyne and Wear
England NE8 1RP

Distributed in South Africa by
KOLLEL BOOKSHOP
22 Muller Street
Yeoville 2198, South Africa

ARTSCROLL HISTORY SERIES®
PILLAR OF FIRE
© *Copyright 1992, by* MESORAH PUBLICATIONS, Ltd.
4401 Second Avenue / Brooklyn, N.Y. 11232 / (718) 921-9000

ISBN
0-89906-847-2 (hard cover)
0-89906-848-0 (paperback)

Typography by Compuscribe at ArtScroll Studios, Ltd.
Printed in the United States of America by Noble Book Press Corp.

◄§ Table of Contents

PILLAR
OF FIRE

CHAPTER ONE

R' Yehoshua Leib's Grandfather — R' Leib Chassid

EATHERED BY THE WINDS and rains of many years, it stands unobtrusively among many others like it on the slopes of the ancient cemetery of Tzefas. Its barely legible letters, eroded by time and the elements, mark the final resting place of the hidden *tzaddik*, R' Leib Chassid.

R' Leib, a direct descendant of *Rashi*, lived most of his life in Slonim, wholly absorbed in the study of Torah. His regimen of seclusion, abstinence and introspection earned him the epithet of "Chassid" which became, with time, part of his name.

As a leading disciple of the Vilna Gaon, R' Leib had his pick of wealthy matches, but he disdained both honor and riches. He declined each prospect without offering any valid reason. No amount of persuasion seemed to have any effect.

Then, one day, the bombshell fell in Slonim: young Leib had become engaged to the poor tailor's daughter.

R' Leib explained his decision with typical simplicity; until then, he had not been ready for marriage. The many offers for excellent matches had been premature. When he decided that the time for marriage had come, he opted to accept the next offer that came his way. And that happened to be the tailor's daughter.

His marriage put the final touch on R' Leib's popular image: a modest, young man with no aspiration in life other than to spend it engrossed in Torah study. He lived for prayer, far removed from worldly concerns, spurning life's amenities. His chosen mate was perfectly suited for a life of poverty, as she raised the couple's two children, Binyamin and Sarah.

Once, the famous R' Yomtov Lipman, head of the rabbinical court of Kapoli and author of *Kedushas Yomtov*, stopped in Slonim on a visit. All the elders and scholars of Slonim went out to the great man to pay their respects. They sought to draw Torah insights from his lips. But he dismissed them with a wave of his hand. "You wish to hear dazzling, original ideas? You wish to sharpen your wits in *pilpul*?" R' Yom Tov asked. "You don't have far to go. Seek out your own R' Leib. He will satisfy your thirst for knowledge."

The scholars of Slonim thought that their visitor was putting them off with a lame excuse, but obeyed him nevertheless. They went to R' Leib. "Our eminent guest, the rav of Kapoli, has sent us to you," they explained.

Out of deference to the town's esteemed guest, R' Leib broke with his custom of not revealing himself except to the narrow circle which had gathered around him. He engaged the scholars of Slonim in an animated discussion. But after having divulged his brilliance this once, R' Leib's customary reticence quickly reasserted itself.

On another occasion, when the same scholars attempted to draw him out again, he responded simply, "I have nothing to say." Reminded of his willingness to engage in Talmudic disputation on that earlier occasion, he replied, "That was only out of respect for the rav of Kapoli."

In 5569 (1809), a deep yearning for the ancestral homeland of the Jewish people, *Eretz Yisrael*, emotionally affected the disciples of the Vilna Gaon, known as *Perushim*. R' Leib, too, was swept up in the

The ancient cemetery of Tzefas

enthusiasm. R' Leib had just betrothed his son, Binyamin, who remained behind in Europe, as R' Leib, his wife and daughter set sail for the Holy Land.

R' Leib and his family sailed on a ship along with R' David Shlomo Eibshitz, *av beis din* of Sarka. R' Leib possessed the only volume of *Gemara* on the ship. In order to allow his esteemed companion to learn, too, he agreed to open up the binding of the precious volume and tear it in two. Thus, R' Leib and R' David Shlomo passed their journey, alternately studying half the volume.

R' Leib settled in the holy city of Tzefas, dwelling place of Kabbalists and mystics. There he lived the same ascetic life he had in Slonim, seeking no recognition of any kind.

The people of Tzefas remained largely unaware of the newcomer in their midst. Once a week, they might see him going out to the fields to greet the Sabbath Bride or sight him praying alone by the tomb of the Ari Hakadosh, but R' Leib did not live long in Tzefas. Soon after his arrival, he died and was buried on the slopes of the ancient cemetery of that holy city.

CHAPTER TWO

R' Yehoshua Leib's Father
— R' Binyamin Diskin

N THE YEAR 5558 (1798), while R' Leib was deeply mourning the death of his master and teacher, the Vilna Gaon, his only son, Binyamin, was born. Though he was to live only forty-six years, R' Binyamin's life was one rich in Torah.

Shortly before he reached the age of *bar mitzvah*, Binyamin was betrothed. At that time, his parents emigrated to *Eretz Yisrael*. However, the few years he had with his father to guide him were sufficient to forge the gifted young boy's character and prepare him for the brilliant future that awaited him.

Later, R' Binyamin would recount how when he was a young boy, his father had been dissatisfied with his diligence in learning. R' Leib swung his son onto his shoulders and brought him to a shoemaker to be apprenticed. The boy quickly realized the implications and begged for a reprieve. That experience left such a deep impression on the boy's tender soul that from then on he threw himself completely into his studies.

Unlike his father, it was Binyamin's destiny to be deeply involved in communal life and activity. Before he reached the age of twenty, he was already *av beis din* and *rosh mesivta* in Horodna.

While still a young man, he was well known beyond the confines of Horodna as a halachic authority and Torah genius. He attracted many brilliant disciples, the most famous of whom were: R' Yitzchak Elchanan Spector, the world-renowned Kovno Rav; R' Shmuel Avigdor, noted author; R' Baruch Mordechai Lifshitz, later rav of Novardhok and Shadlitz; and R' Shabsai of Piesk.

In addition to his most famous son, R' Yehoshua Leib, universally known as the Brisker Rav, Binyamin's three other sons were also scholars of note: R' Avraham Shmuel, author of *Livnei Binyamin* and *av beis din* of Plonsk and Valkovisk; R' Zorach, rav of Horodna; and R' Noach Yitzchak, *av beis din* of Lomza.

R' Binyamin suffered his whole life from a sickly constitution. His chronic weakness prevented him from recording his many *chiddushim*. However, when it came to lecturing to his students, his overpowering love of Torah would infuse his infirm bones with incredible vigor. His son testified that "his father counted the minutes from one *shiur* to the next."

R' BINYAMIN WAS CONSTANTLY prodding and encouraging others to maintain a steady learning schedule. He was fond of quoting

No Jewish Organization Without Torah Learning

his father, who had heard from his father, that every Jewish society or organization should enforce specific rules binding its members to learn a specific amount of *Gemara* or *Mishnah* daily. In his days, even the *chevrah kadisha* would divide the learning of the entire Talmud among its members.

R' Binyamin's principle, that no Jewish organization should be formed which did not include in its charter a requirement that all members learn a fixed amount daily, was many decades later relied upon by his son R' Yehoshua Leib to resolve a thorny problem in Jerusalem. Christian missionaries were then actively disseminating their poison among the Jerusalem populace. The poverty of the populace, constantly hovering on the verge of starvation, made many susceptible to the missionaries' lures. Frequent epidemics left a trail of destitute widows and orphans.

The widespread suffering provided the missionaries with the opportunity to exhibit their "Christian mercy" in the form of material help. The missionaries established a hospital, which offered the best doctors and most expensive medicines free of charge. People found themselves faced with choosing between life and death, since there was no other hospital offering medical care — even for a price.

R' Yehoshua Leib Diskin

R' Avraham Chaim Gogin, the *Chacham Bashi* (the government-authorized Sephardic chief rabbi), fought the missionaries with all his might. Once, he became seriously ill and there was no doctor in the entire city aside from the one employed in the missionary hospital. The rabbi's family wanted to bring him there to be treated, but R' Avraham Chaim adamantly refused and eventually succumbed to the disease.

A few activists eventually established an organization which they called "Bnei Yisrael," whose purpose was to fight missionary activity tooth and nail. The leaders of "Bnei Yisrael" found that they had to join forces with non-religious elements who had considerable influence with high officials in the Turkish administration.

One evening, R' Yeshaya Orenstein paid R' Yehoshua Leib Diskin a visit. He entered, removed his shoes and sat on the ground like a mourner. When the rav asked him what had happened, R' Yeshaya replied that he was lamenting the downfall of Jerusalem Jewry. He then told R' Yehoshua Leib about "Bnei Yisrael's" alliance with non-religious elements. Who knows, he wept, what could eventually result from such a union? R' Yehoshua Leib promised to look into the matter and see what could be done.

As soon as R' Yeshaya left his home, R' Yehoshua Leib sent for one of the officials of the organization, R' Nachum Levi, and asked him about the purpose of the society. R' Nachum described the inroads being made by the missionaries in snaring Jewish souls and how, to meet this threat, "Bnei Yisrael" had joined forces with those with influence in high places.

"We have a tradition handed down from our elders, the elderly scholars in Brisk," the rav began, "not to establish any fraternal society aside from a study group such as a *Chevras Shas* or *Chevras Mishnayos.* Any group which is not based on Torah is subject to the influence of alien elements, who eventually undermine its very purpose. Even the members of the burial society in Brisk were obligated to attend a daily *shiur.* I therefore advise you that if you wish to continue this organization, you must impose upon all of its members the duty of participating in a daily *Gemara shiur.* Whoever refuses to adhere to this regulation should be removed from the society."

The founders of "Bnei Yisrael" promulgated this amendment and before long, the secular elements had dropped out.

R' BINYAMIN DID NOT CONFINE his lectures and teaching to his *yeshivah;* halachic queries came to him from distant places also. Great

Judgment by Lot

leaders of the generation sought his counsel in important matters.

Two men once appeared before him for a *din Torah.* He ruled that both must swear, but could not decide which one should swear first. Finally, R' Binyamin chose to settle the matter by lots. R' Yitzchak Elchanan Spector happened to be visiting Horodna at the time. He heard some of the local scholars belittling R' Binyamin's method of using lots. They considered such an apparently chance resolution to be inappropriate for resolving a *din Torah.* R' Yitzchak Elchanan, a youth of eighteen, defended his teacher by opening up the *Shulchan Aruch* and showing them an identical ruling of the *Taz.* The scoffers were abashed at having been bested by one of R' Binyamin's youngest disciples.

R' Binyamin was besieged by many *agunos,* women whose husbands had disappeared and who were unable to remarry. Many of these women had already approached other rabbis who granted them permission to remarry conditional upon R' Binyamin's signature.

In 5591 (1830), he ordered that a body be disinterred and identified before the "widow" was permitted to remarry. (His son, R' Yehoshua Leib, later followed a similar procedure in a case that came before him in Jerusalem). On another occasion, R' Shmuel Salant referred an exceedingly complex *agunah* question to R' Binyamin.

DESPITE HIS HEAVY INVOLVEMENT in giving *shiurim*, writing responsa and seeing to communal matters, R' Binyamin nevertheless

Rebbe to His Sons

managed to establish regular study sessions with his children, whom he educated himself. This took up a considerable part of his day.

His son testifies to this in his introduction to *Livnei Yosef*:

> We know that the spirit of our father speaks within us and his word is ever upon our lips. For from the time we were able to speak, until the very end of his days, our father did not let us be educated by any other teacher. We drank our fill from his pure well of knowledge.

R' Binyamin reveled in the time he spent teaching his children. One *erev Yom Kippur*, before sundown, when the townspeople were all streaming to the synagogue for *Kol Nidrei*, the rabbi still had not come. When it began getting dark, they sent the *shammash* to R' Binyamin's house to see what was detaining him. The *shammash* entered and found the rabbi studying with his young son, Yehoshua Leib.

R' Binyamin explained the delay. Having examined his deeds of the past year, he had found himself sorely lacking, empty of *mitzvos* and worthy deeds. How could he usher in the awesome day in such a state? He had seized the first *mitzvah* that came to his mind, *veshinantam levanecha* — to teach your son — hoping that with this merit he would be able to face his Maker on *Yom Kippur*.

R' Binyamin was steeped in study and teaching. But communal matters also made demands upon him and impinged upon his precious time. Before he lent his attention to any communal affair, he would examine it thoroughly to see if it justified leaving his Torah study.

WHEN HE DID DEVOTE HIMSELF to the public, he revealed himself to be a man guided by Divine spirit.

A Pointed Mashal He was once compelled to speak at a celebration feting Napoleon after his liberation of Poland from Russian rule. One evening, without advance notice, armed guards appeared in R' Binyamin's home to take him to a celebration being held in Napoleon's honor. He only learned of his destination along the way.

The royal ballroom was dazzlingly illuminated and ornately decorated. R' Binyamin found himself in the presence of the aristocracy of the land, as well as bishops and archbishops. A priest was in the midst of a flowery speech about the Polish nation and the great conqueror, and his lengthy address gave R' Binyamin a little time to orient himself and organize his own thoughts. He sought to avoid empty flattery and feared that an excess of blandishment of the Polish nobility might arouse the peasants against the Jews.

When R' Binyamin's turn finally came, he began by describing the ways of the Creator, which at first appear mysterious and perplexing, but when contemplated deeply, are revealed as perfect.

Consider the story of Joseph, a pure soul languishing in jail. Not only had he suffered at the hands of his own brothers when they sold him into slavery, he had also been falsely accused and thrown into prison.

If Divine Providence ordained greatness for him, why was it necessary for him to suffer this degradation? Why was his life so embittered? R' Binyamin explained that G-d wanted someone, who would one day have the power to punish and pardon, to first taste the bitterness of suffering and imprisonment. He had to experience in a physical and emotional sense the injustice and inequality. Later, when he became the leader of men, he would know what it meant to be falsely accused and how it felt to be imprisoned. He would sympathize with men brought before him for trial and would think carefully before he meted out punishment.

An insight into Joseph's situation may also explain why the Polish nation had suffered. The Creator knew that this nation was destined for a greater role, that it would soon rule other nations and extend its protection to other peoples. That is why Divine Providence saw fit to give it a foretaste of injustice and oppression.

"Let me tell you a story," R' Binyamin continued, "to illustrate how power can corrupt one who has not tasted suffering in his life and how such a person relates to the miserable victims whose life he controls.

"Once, there was a young Polish nobleman who owned many estates which he leased to Jewish tenants. He found these Jews easy targets for his crazy whims.

"One wintry evening, the count was restless. He tossed uneasily upon his bed until he finally summoned his valet and said, 'I am unable to sleep tonight. Let's wake up the Jewish tenants on my property and have some sport.' He got dressed and took his wife along for the fun.

"They reached the first stop on their nocturnal itinerary. The driver climbed down from his perch and knocked upon the door of the Jewish tenant's home, shouting, 'The count and countess have come to honor you with a visit.' The entire household was roused and began bustling about to prepare a suitable welcome for the noble guests. They lit all the lamps, spread a white tablecloth on the table and emptied the pantry of any food fit to serve aristocracy.

"The count sat down at the head of the table and surveyed the lavish spread before him while the Jewish inhabitants cowered fearfully in the corner. The count glared at his host and said, 'Everything seems to be in order here except for one thing. I don't see any Swiss cheese on the table. I am so fond of it, you know!' The Jew began stammering that he had not been informed of the count's visit and had not known to prepare that delicacy in advance. The count refused to be appeased. He demanded Swiss cheese. If his wish were not fulfilled at once, the Jew would be flogged. No amount of pleading helped. The Jew was stretched out on the floor and whipped until blood coursed down his back. The Jew's wife and children whimpered helplessly from their corner, but their plight only increased the count's mirth.

"The wife of the Jew had the quick wits to send one of her children off to her neighbors and warn them that their landlord was on his way to pay a visit and that he craved Swiss cheese.

"The count finally left the first home and continued on. He stopped off at the next house on the road and found the table already set with tempting delicacies, including Swiss cheese.

"He studied the scene and said, 'But where is the Tokay wine?'

"The Jew apologized that he had been caught by surprise. But the count would not be mollified and that tenant, too, was stretched out and lashed to within an inch of his life.

"The third household was duly warned of the approaching visit of the count and countess. The Jew was told to prepare Swiss cheese and Tokay wine to please his noble guest.

"As soon as the Jew heard the rumbling of the wagon wheels and the tinkling of the horses' bells, he ran out and invited the count in. 'Please do us the honor of gracing our humble home with a visit,' he begged.

"The Jew stepped aside and let his distinguished guests enter before him. To the count's amazement, the table was bare. The tenant then turned to his landlord and explained, 'I know that anything I do will fail to please you because all you want is an excuse to have sport with me. So I am sparing you the trouble of wracking your brain to think up excuses. Here is my back, Your Excellency. Do with it what you will.'

"The count was insulted by this blunt declaration and suddenly lost all taste for this form of entertainment. Turning around, he shamefacedly left and returned to his mansion."

R' Binyamin paused, then gazed about at his audience. "If this miserable Jew had not prepared a biting repartee for the count, his fate would have been the same as his two predecessors and he would have been victim to the same blows.

"How are we to understand the count's fiendish whim? It can only be grasped in the light of his background and upbringing. The count was spoiled from birth. He had never been beaten or flogged. He never felt pain and never saw people around him suffering. Thus, he was insensitive to the pain of the first two Jews.

"G-d rules and conducts His world through mercy. He treats His creatures with loving kindness," said R' Binyamin, directing his gaze at the noblemen seated all around. "He imposed the rule of the

Russians upon the Polish nation so that they would have a taste of suffering and oppression. This would teach the members of our nation to sympathize with the downtrodden and the subjugated, and to feel for them as they had felt themselves. Let us hope that, as in the story, the noblemen here will lose their taste for violence and blood, that they will find no sport in persecuting those who are weak and helpless. Let us truly hope that our nation has been trained and prepared for independence and liberty, and that they will let all of its citizens enjoy the same freedom."

His speech had a powerful impact upon its audience. It reflected the festive aspect of the event while shedding light upon the difficult plight of his fellow Jews who were subjected to the capricious tyranny of the aristocrats seated in that very hall. A hush fell over the audience. R' Binyamin was escorted home with a royal guard.

R' BINYAMIN WAS OFFERED another opportunity to appear before exalted officials and plead for his people. In 5600 (1840), Lithuanian

Reluctant Emissary Jewry was ordered to choose a representative to appear at a conference convened by the government in St. Petersburg. The *Tzemach Tzedek* of Lubavitch was chosen to represent the *chassidim* and R' Binyamin to represent Lithuanian Jewry.

When he heard of his appointment, R' Binyamin acquired a doctor's letter attesting that he was too ill to travel and R' Itzele Volozhiner, son of R' Chaim Volozhiner, was chosen instead. One of his close acquaintances, suspecting that R' Binyamin was shirking the responsibility, visited him and asked him how he could ignore the needs of his people.

R' Binyamin explained: "I am certain that the representative we send to St. Petersburg will not be consulted upon any religious matter and asked for his opinion. Rather, we will be asked to sign our agreement to a finished document. If I knew that the matter in question was of the nature of *yehareg ve'al yaavor* — something for which we must give up our lives, rather than transgress — I would know exactly what to do. But I fear that the government wants our signature upon measures which might appear on the surface to be harmless. In this event, I would be tempted to sign, even against my better judgment. The harmful implications might only become apparent fifty or a hundred years hence, but I would be to blame. I would regret having signed such a measure and be doomed forever. This is what has prompted me to evade going and committing myself."

JUST AS HIS STEPS AND ACTS were carefully measured when it came to public matters, so it was in his personal life. R' Binyamin was

The Difference Revealed

extremely scrupulous in everything he did. He was strict with himself on all halachic questions. If the hint of a question ever arose concerning the *kashrus* of some food or drink, he would abstain from it altogether even if it were proven kosher. Anything that reached his mouth was sifted and examined countless times.

His eldest son, R' Yehoshua Leib, noticed as a boy that whenever a question arose concerning any food being prepared in the house, even if the food was ruled permissible in the end, it would be served to the children but not to R' Binyamin. Little Yehoshua Leib took this as a personal affront. If R' Binyamin deemed a dish unsuitable for himself, why should he allow his children to eat it? Why should he be more demanding of himself than of his own children?

Sometime later, a fire erupted in a village near Valkovisk, where the family lived. It spread to the synagogue and partially scorched the Torah scrolls in the *aron kodesh*. When the fire was extinguished, the villagers sent a messenger to R' Binyamin to ask what to do.

The messenger, bearing the singed Torah scrolls in his arms, was ushered into the rabbi's home by young Yehoshua Leib, who asked him what had happened. The villager described the fire and its devastating results. Yehoshua Leib led the villager into his father's study at once.

When R' Binyamin saw the blackened parchments in the man's arms, he fainted. The man raised a cry of alarm and the family, rushing to R' Binyamin's side, succeeded in reviving him, after much effort. However, it still took some time before R' Binyamin could compose himself sufficiently to deal with the villager's problem. "From then on," R' Yehoshua Leib recalled, "I no longer had any complaints against my father. I clearly saw the difference between him and me."

R' Binyamin had so purified himself that he could not understand how people could live a life without Torah. He used to say that had he not seen a wicked man with his own eyes, he would not have been able to conceive of such a possibility.

THE VERY EPISODES WHICH illustrate his piety and righteousness also illuminate his deep modesty. As a rabbi in Lomza, he was

A Vow Annulled confronted with a problem: a Torah scholar had vowed never to leave the four walls of the *beis medrash*. The Jewish community provided him with his meals but this constant burden soon became more than the *askanim* could bear. *Shabbos* and festivals were especially difficult, since there was no *eruv* and the food had to be brought in advance. The members of the community sought a solution to their dilemma.

At that time, R' Akiva Eiger happened to pass through Lomza and he stopped by to pay his respects to R' Binyamin, who broached the matter of the cloistered scholar who refused to leave the *beis medrash* and who had become an intolerable burden upon the good people of the community. The two *gedolim* discussed the problem and arrived at a solution.

They left R' Binyamin's house and headed for the *beis medrash*. Whoever saw these two distinguished personalities was moved to follow respectfully behind. Soon a huge procession had formed, headed by the two eminent rabbis. They entered the *beis medrash* and approached the sequestered scholar, saying, "We have heard that you are a noteworthy Torah scholar and, since you swore not to leave this place, we decided to come and visit you here."

The man was deeply pained at having caused such great Torah luminaries such trouble. Seeing his discomfort, they asked him, "Had you known that we would visit you, would you still have made your vow?"

"G-d forbid!" he exclaimed with alacrity. "I would never have imposed on you and made you go to such trouble! I would never have made my vow to begin with!"

The two great men nodded and said, "In that case, you are absolved of your vow." And the people all echoed, *"Mutar lach, mutar lach, mutar lach* — your vow has been annulled."

ONE *SHABBOS*, ONE OF the laymen in his city, a simple businessman, paid R' Binyamin a visit and told him, in detail, about a

The Rav Knew

business trip which he planned for the morrow. R' Binyamin listened silently, but whenever the man uttered the word "riding," R' Binyamin gently corrected the verb to "walking."

The following day, the businessman arrived at the coach only to learn that it had just departed. He ran to the next stop hoping to overtake it, but he again missed it by a few minutes. He continued on foot to the third stop but again, the coach had already gone. Seeing that he had already covered half the distance, he decided to walk the rest of the way. As he was walking along the road, he recalled the conversation of the previous day. It suddenly dawned upon him that whenever he had used the word "riding," the rabbi had amended it to "walking."

He later returned to R' Binyamin and told him how the rabbi's words had been fulfilled and he had been forced to walk the entire distance. R' Binyamin shrugged the matter off, saying, "I only corrected you because, according to the *halachah*, it is forbidden on *Shabbos* to speak of plans to travel in a vehicle. I meant nothing more."

ON HIS WAY TO THE SYNAGOGUE one morning, R' Binyamin came across a Jewish porter puffing and panting under a heavy load. R'

Faithful Partners / Unfaithful Partners

Binyamin stopped, helped remove the burden from the man's back, and then hoisted it onto his own. As if the porter's partner, he then carried the pack all the way to the man's destination.

Another time, two wealthy partners entrusted a large sum of money to R' Binyamin. Some time later, one of the partners came to claim part of the money, saying that a business opportunity had arisen for which he needed cash. R' Binyamin refused to give him the sum he required.

"Don't you trust me?" the man shouted angrily. He ranted against the rabbi. R' Binyamin calmed him down and explained, "Of course, I trust you. But what can I do if your partner came to me yesterday with the same request?"

When the man heard this, he screamed aloud, "What! My partner took the money? What a scoundrel! What a swindler! And you believed him? You gave him the money?"

R' Binyamin smiled. "Rest assured. Did I say that I gave him any money? G-d forbid. I would not do such a thing. I can only return the money to both of you together." Suddenly the man realized what he had been asking. He bowed his head in shame and begged the rabbi's pardon.

THE RESIDENTS OF LOMZA became jealous of those of Horodna and Valkovisk, the cities in which R' Binyamin served as rav and *av beis*

His Legacy *din*, and succeeded in wooing him to their city. But R' Binyamin did not serve there long. In *Adar* 5604 (1844), R' Binyamin passed away, to the grief of all Jewry.

His many disciples dispersed, returning to their homes bearing the accumulated Torah knowledge they had amassed from R' Binyamin and marked by the purity which they had acquired under his tutelage. Many of them became great rabbis in the most illustrious Jewish communities of Europe.

The fire which R' Binyamin kindled in the hearts of his disciples did not flicker and his teachings illuminated their way for scores of years to come. Perhaps his greatest student was R' Yitzchak Elchanan Spector, the Kovno Rav.

An outstanding example of his disciples' implicit trust in R' Binyamin and their dependence upon his judgment can be seen from the example of R' Yitzchak Elchanan. The latter was a devout

R' Yitzchock Elchanan Spector

student of R' Binyamin and served him faithfully in his youth. When R' Yitzchak Elchanan completed his monumental *Be'er Yitzchak*, he refused to release it until he traveled all the way to Lomza to prostrate himself upon the grave of his master and to beg permission to publish his work.

Each year on his *yahrzeit*, R' Binyamin's disciples would gather to pray at his graveside in Lomza. The tomb was also visited by many whose lives were embittered by suffering. They came to pour out their hearts by the grave of this saintly man and beg him to intercede for them in Heaven.

R' ELIYAHU DAVID RABINOWITZ, the author of *HaAderess*, tells the following moving story about R' Binyamin:

A Blessing Fulfilled R' Binyamin Diskin, rav of Horodna, led his flock with a firm and wise hand. He was held in great esteem by all. The members of the local *beis din* had their own room in R' Binyamin's house while he sat and learned in an inner room. All halachic questions or arguments were first brought to the *beis din*. When the *dayanim* failed to arrive at a solution, they

Remnants of the cemetery of Lomza. Right: the grave of R' Binyamin Diskin. Left: the grave of R' Shlomoh Zalman Chassid, first Lomzer Rav.

would approach the rav; but aside from the members of the *beis din*, no one had access to the rav's inner study.

One day, a splendid coach rolled up before the rav's house. An elegantly dressed woman dismounted and presented herself to the *beis din* as a stranger from Prussia. A most urgent matter had brought her to the rav, a matter which she was not at liberty to divulge to anyone but him.

The rav was sitting in his study at a table piled high with heavy tomes. Standing humbly across from him, she softly begged his forgiveness for disturbing him. She introduced herself as a woman who, although living in "enlightened" Germany, was considered one of the most devout women in her city. She maintained a home of the most impeccable standards.

Then, lowering her voice, she confessed that she was the daughter of the infamous author of *Nesivos Olam*, a five-volume work which had first appeared in London. Caustically written, dripping with venom, by an apostate and containing highly distorted information about Judaism and both the Written and Oral Torah, it shocked anyone who merely glimpsed through it.

Originally published in both Hebrew and English versions, *Nesivos Olam* was widely circulated throughout England and set off shock waves. English Jewry was up in arms against it, and Sir Moses Montefiore, the great Jewish philanthropist, called an assembly of all prominent Jewish figures. At the time, Montefiore was about to embark upon a voyage to Damascus on behalf of its Jewish community, which lay under the shadow of a blood libel. He planned to go from there to meet with Czar Nicholas to beg him to revoke some of his harsh decrees against Russian Jewry.

The meeting in England was stormy. People denounced this renegade who had so besmirched the name of Jewry with his hateful lies. Montefiore undertook to search for a clever, learned Jew, with a gifted pen, who would be able to rebut the dastardly accusations which appeared in *Nesivos Olam*.

The woman told R' Binyamin that her father had been a *melamed* in a Lithuanian village in his young years. Rumors began to circulate that he was lax in his observance. Even though he was a very capable teacher, parents began withdrawing their children from his tutelage. When he found himself without any source of income, he left home to seek another means of livelihood.

At first, he wrote occasional letters home to his wife to let her know where he was. But when he stopped writing, many conflicting rumors arose concerning his whereabouts and his activities. People said that he had gone to London, where he had been taken under the wing of missionaries and converted to Christianity.

His wife remained an *agunah*. The townspeople took pity on her and her only daughter, and supported them out of the charity coffers.

In time, the financial condition of the deserted wife improved and she became wealthy. She maintained a decent, respectable home and raised her daughter to be a fine Jewish girl. The daughter grew up and married a young scholar of upstanding character. The new couple moved to Germany and established a proper Jewish home.

This daughter labored to efface all memories of her disgraced father. Any reminder of him pained her deeply. She was, therefore, shocked to receive a letter one day which bore the name and return address of her father, the *meshumad*. It took a monumental effort on her part to overcome the aversion she felt and open the letter. She finally did and read:

> Dear Daughter,
>
> I am well aware of my lowly stature and worthlessness in your eyes and in the eyes of the entire Jewish people. I am also aware of the terrible sin which I committed against G-d, His Torah and His people. But I also want you to know, my daughter, that in the end, after having sunk deep into the morass of iniquity, the spark of Jewishness in me has reawakened. Remorse now gnaws away at my entire being; it gives me no surcease from pain or suffering. I cannot rest. My friends — my fellow hatemongers and missionaries who brought me to my lowly state and who used me shamefully for their evil ends to besmirch the Jewish people, the Torah and the Almighty — have since abandoned me. They used me while they could, but when they saw that I had outlived my usefulness and had begun to repent, they began oppressing me and eventually expelled me from their midst.

I am now old and sick, a shattered potsherd, both in spirit and body. I am an outcast, a pariah, shunned by all. I have no one to turn to, no place to go, nowhere to lay down my weary head. Dear daughter, I beg of you, have pity on your forsaken father. Help me out of my terrible plight. I ask of you no more than a little corner in your house to repose my head and to live out the remaining years which G-d has granted me in this world.

"This letter threw me into a turmoil," the elegant woman confessed. "I spoke the matter over with my husband. He advised me to reply as follows:

"We are ready to allow you into our home on the condition that you dress yourself as a Jew and comport yourself as one. Also, during your stay under our roof, you are not to speak to anyone outside the house or to breathe a word of your past. We want you to cause us no unnecessary shame."

The father had agreed to all of their demands. With a remorseful heart and a spirit wracked with pain, he had made his way to her home. As soon as he opened the door, he had burst into a deluge of tears. Rivers upon rivers flowed from his eyes until he fell exhausted to the ground.

The members of the family carried him to a bed in the room set aside for him. He lay there, his head whirling, his heart pounding and his eyes shedding an endless stream of tears. He must have felt as if his tears were helping, somewhat, to wash away the terrible sins of his lifetime.

He wasted away quickly, finding no peace for his restless spirit. Ashamed to look his daughter and son-in-law in the eye, he sat by the window all day, looking out at the chirping birds.

Sometimes, he would get up and pace the room, his lips trembling as he murmured, "Before Whom must you give an accounting . . ." He would begin shuddering from head to toe. Scenes of his lifetime would swim before his eyes and he would burst into bitter, frightful cries, which continued until he fell down in a faint and was laid to bed. He would burrow his head into the pillow, ashamed of raising it even to look at the walls of his room.

One day in *Elul*, he felt that his end was near. He called for his daughter and son-in-law. When they stood before him, he whispered weakly, "Dear children, I want to convey my last will and testament through which I hope that my unbearable burden of sins will find one good advocate in the person of some great Jewish leader to whom you will tell my life-story."

"I want you to know, my dear ones, that our family originated in Altona. R' Yehonasan Eibshitz served as rav there when I was born. A great controversy raged then between him and R' Yaakov Emden, who accused him of consorting with the heretical followers of Shabsai Tzvi.

"R' Yaakov Emden maintained a *minyan* in his house, since the community trustees prohibited him from setting foot in the central synagogue due to his strong opposition to the rav. This *minyan* was also attended by people who nursed petty personal animosities against the rav and who joined with R' Yaakov Emden to vent their grievances. My father was among this group, and being especially gifted with the pen, lent his talents to fan the flames of the controversy. He wrote pamphlets denouncing the rav.

"He once wrote a pamphlet which he called *Akitzas Akrav*. It was published on the very day of my *bris*. All the people attending the services wished him a double *mazel tov* and noted that it was a propitious omen that both joyous occasions fell on one day. R' Yaakov Emden raised his hand to command the people's attention and said, 'I would like to wish our esteemed author a hearty *mazel tov*. I pray that in the merit of his efforts his child should grow up to be exactly the opposite of the man against whom his pamphlet is aimed. May his parents enjoy great *nachas* from him.'

"Everyone chimed in 'Amen.'

"When they told the rav about this feast and about the blessing which had been conferred upon the newborn, R' Yehonasan's face flamed a bright red and he blurted out, 'So be it! Amen!' "

A deep sigh escaped the old man's throat, making him pause in sad reminiscence. Then he continued, "Now you can understand, my dear ones, the curse that hovered over my life. We all realize now that both men were justified, for both R' Yehonasan and R' Yaakov were righteous and holy men. And since both of them 'blessed' me that I should grow up to be the exact opposite of the *tzaddik* R' Yehonasan, this pronouncement was fulfilled to the letter. A force beyond my control coerced me into seeking the path which led me to the lowest abyss. I don't mean to offer this as an excuse for my dastardly actions or to exonerate myself from blame. I deserve the punishment that awaits me. But I do hope that what I have just said will mitigate it. The blessing I received as an eight-day-old infant turned into a curse which overshadowed my entire life, both in this world and the World to Come. But if you tell my sorry tale to one of the righteous men of this generation and importune him to pray for my sinful soul, I hope that after my tainted soul is purged in the fires of *Gehinnom* for the punishment it richly deserves, it will find some peace. For the Almighty Himself promised that no one shall be forever cast out."

When the old man finished speaking, he fell back upon his pillows and lay there motionless. Then, suddenly, he leaped up. His eyes had a wild, frantic look, as if he was looking for a way to escape. He began shrieking hysterically, "*Gevald! Gevald!* — Help! Help!"

"What is the matter, Father?" the two asked him in alarm.

"Woe unto me! I fear the Day of Judgment! I fear the Day of Rebuke!" he shouted from the depths of his heart.

He turned a deathly pale and began breathing laboriously. His head fell back on the pillows and with a cry of "*Shema Yisrael*," he breathed his last.

The rav of Horodna, R' Binyamin Diskin, had been listening to this account with rapt attention. He promised the woman that he would do all he could to repair her father's damaged soul and secure him an everlasting peace. She thanked him profusely and left.

The *dayanim* of the *beis din*, who had been sitting in the adjoining room, were surprised that the rav, whose time was so precious, had sat so patiently listening to the long story of a stranger.

When she left the room, the rav went out to them and said, "You must surely be wondering why I agreed to listen to this long story, especially from a woman whom I did not know. Let me tell you what I just heard so that it may serve as a poignant lesson of how terrible is controversy and how careful one must be to keep away from anything that smacks of disrespect to the Torah."

He then repeated the long story he had just heard. In conclusion, he said, "We clearly see the bitter end of what began as diatribes against a great person for the glory of Heaven. Denouncing *tzaddikim* is like playing with fire; no one emerges unscathed. Praiseworthy is the person who stands back and refrains from taking any part in such controversy, which must, necessarily, cause dishonor to the Torah. Fortunate is one who does not become involved in shameful dissension."

CHAPTER THREE

R' Yehoshua Leib's Childhood

ORODNA. THE TENTH of *Kislev* 5577 (1817).
A pelting rain flooded the city, accompanied by hail and frost. People huddled in their homes behind shuttered win-
His Birth dows, and even the poorest hovels had stoves burning.
In the home of R' Binyamin, the *av beis din*, there was a festive air,
for a baby boy had just come into the world. The infant's father sat at
the head of a table, engrossed in study. The fireplace at his right shed
warmth and light. The door of the house creaked continually as it
swung open and shut to admit the dignitaries and scholars of the city,
the *askanim* and the simple lay folk. All came to offer warm
congratulations to their beloved rav. One group came and another left.

On the seventeenth day of the month, R' Binyamin initiated his
infant son into the covenant of Avraham Avinu. Everyone in the city
turned out to participate in the joyous event. Little did they realize that
this tender child, who was named Yehoshua Yehudah Leib, would
become the undisputed leader of his generation.

This infant was immediately immersed into the world of Torah. His
cradle remained by his father's side, in a house that was as much a *beis
medrash* as it was a dwelling. The air vibrated with the sound of

study. The baby's tiny ears absorbed the sounds of the "controversies of Abaye and Rava" which filled the house.

Of his childhood, little is known. The people of Horodna applied to the child the insight of *Chazal*, concerning Moshe Rabbeinu. It is written, "And Moshe grew up," upon which *Chazal* ask, "Don't all children grow up?" *Chazal* answer that the Torah wishes to indicate that Moshe matured at a different rate than the rest of the world.

R' Binyamin hired a *melamed*, R' Moshe Horodner (who later settled in Jerusalem), to teach the boy *aleph-beis*. After he was fluent in the alphabet, the boy came under his father's tutelage. R' Binyamin wished to be the sole influence in his son's education. Indeed, he was the first to recognize the boy's exceptional talents and superhuman will power. Whatever the world was later to hail as outstanding in R' Yehoshua Leib, his father already recognized in the boy's early years.

R' BINYAMIN ONCE TOOK a walk with his young son in the woods. As they were strolling along, the father said, "My son, you should

The Insights of a Child

know that *Hashem* is unique. He is One and Only."

The boy nodded in understanding. He was aware of this. It needed no explanation.

His father looked at Yehoshua Leib in surprise, as if to ask, "How do you know that this is so self-evident?"

The boy replied in childlike naivete, "Did you not tell me a few days ago that *Hashem*'s glory fills the entire earth? If this is so, then there is no room for anything besides Him, and He is One and Only!"

When Yehoshua Leib was a lad, the *shammash* in the city organized a raffle for some item of value. He sold the numbered tickets and inserted the stubs into a box where they were shaken about. The single ticket drawn was the winning number.

After the lottery had taken place, the *shammash* discarded the box and let the children play with it. Someone shook out all the folded tickets and pretended to hold a mock drawing. In the process, it was discovered that one number appeared twice.

Little Yehoshua Leib then announced that the drawing had been invalid. The children paid no attention. The boy then turned to the adults and repeated his claim that the lottery should be disqualified. They reassured him that it made no difference any more since the owner of the double ticket had not won.

But the boy refused to give in. He maintained that the lottery must be drawn again. He explained his reasoning hypothetically: What if the man whose number appeared twice had, in fact, won the drawing? Then they would surely have invalidated the entire drawing since it was not right for him to have had a double chance. It thus followed that the man with the double number had altogether forfeited his chance of winning, which was not fair. "And what if the *shammash* had omitted one number?" he asked the men who had gathered around him. "Would you not demand a new drawing, just as well? Why is this case different, then?"

The adults nodded their heads in agreement with his unshakable logic.

A particular clock was always slow, until one day it broke down altogether. When he saw this, young Yehoshua Leib rejoiced.

"Why are you so happy that the clock broke down?" people asked him. He explained, "Until now, the clock never gave the right time. Now, the clock will tell the correct time twice a day."

Two young men sat in his father's *beis medrash* one evening, arguing about what to study. One wished to study a tractate connected to *Yoreh Deah* while the other wished to study a tractate in *Nezikin*.

They were still debating the issue when the rav's son entered. They decided to ask him to mediate and promised to abide by his decision.

The boy listened gravely to their points and then arbitrated: "If you study the chapter *Eizehu Neshech* [a tractate in *Bava Metzia* dealing with interest, the laws of which are found in *Yoreh Deah*], you will both be satisfied!"

WHEN HE WAS FIVE, Yehoshua Leib became seriously ill. R' Binyamin summoned the townspeople and pleaded with them to pray for the

The Young Prodigy

recovery of "the genius of the generation who is about to die." The people looked at him in wonder. Who was he referring to? He explained, "I mean my little son."

The people prayed intensely and little Yehoshua Leib recovered.

According to R' Yitzchak Elchanan, little Yehoshua Leib was the most outstanding of his father's students, even when he was a mere boy. Before he had reached *bar mitzvah* age, he was already teaching a *shiur* in *Poskim*.

R' Arye Leib Frumkin writes: "R' Yitzchak Elchanan would often tell me how he befriended R' Yehoshua Leib in his father's house. The boy was a prodigy and wonder, like the sun at its zenith, even in his early years."

Once, a rav in one of the outlying towns erred in a certain halachic ruling. The townspeople came before R' Binyamin, demanding that he be deposed.

R' Binyamin asked to meet the rav to see if they were justified in demanding his resignation. He invited the rav to his house and asked him to explain his false ruling. The rav admitted that he had erred and that there was no loophole to justify his mistaken ruling. R' Binyamin was surprised to hear such an outright admission. He rebuked him severely for having misled the public in such a serious matter.

The rav left his presence, bowed and contrite.

R' Yehoshua Leib, then under thirteen at the time, was overcome with pity for the rav. He rushed over to him and asked him in what way he had ruled incorrectly.

The rav, fighting to contain his tears, told the boy how he had ruled mistakenly. "Now I will have to forfeit my position," he wept. "I don't know how I will support my family."

R' Yehoshua Leib tried to calm the rav with soft, reassuring words. Then he asked him to return the following day; he hoped by then to have an idea to help him.

R' Yehoshua Leib secluded himself in his room that night, but he did not go to sleep. He concentrated all of his mental powers on analyzing the problem. He finally succeeded in finding a way to justify the rav's ruling.

He wrote down his findings and, early the next morning, presented it to the rav. The latter copied it over in his own handwriting and brought it into R' Binyamin. Then he left, without waiting for R' Binyamin to discuss the matter with him.

R' Binyamin studied the paper before him and marveled at the brilliant logic behind it. It truly shed a new light on the matter. He was so astonished that during his daily *shiur*, he reviewed the matter with is students. He told them, "They say that you are excellent scholars with brilliant minds. Know that in an obscure village not far from here there is a humble rav whose expertise in Torah far outstrips yours!"

He went on to describe the details of the ruling and how the rav had defended his position. The students listened and were beside themselves with amazement. The only indifferent one was Yehoshua Leib. This was especially strange, in view of his usual enthusiasm in grappling with intricate halachic problems. R' Binyamin fixed his son with a penetrating stare and suddenly deduced that he had lent a hand in this matter.

ON ANOTHER OCCASION, an *agunah* in Valkovisk came to R' Binyamin with a document permitting her to remarry. It was signed by R' Dov

An Agunah Saved

Berish Ashkenazi, *av beis din* of Slonim, but contingent upon the signature of other great authorities. The woman begged R' Binyamin to sign the document which would free her to remarry. R' Binyamin was preoccupied at the moment and asked the woman to wait in an adjoining room and show the documents to his son for inspection.

She peeked into the window of the adjoining room and saw a young lad seated by a large *Gemara*. "There is only some young *bachur'l* in the other room," she said, returning to R' Binyamin.

He nodded. "I know. He is the one I had in mind."

The woman hesitated to give the boy her important documents upon which her entire future depended. But she finally did. As the young lad was flipping through the papers, one page tore.

The woman burst into tears. Were all her efforts to be in vain? R' Binyamin rushed into the room. Seeing the torn sheet and realizing that it was his son's fault, R' Binyamin scolded the lad.

Yehoshua Leib was filled with remorse and promised that he would arrange a new set of papers for her, which would be conclusive in halachically releasing her from her *agunah* status.

He fulfilled his promise and secured a full release. R' Binyamin later wrote a pamphlet dealing with the matter. It opens with the words: "My astute and famous son undertook the writ for a certain woman . . ."

SLOWLY BUT SURELY, the boy's prodigious powers came to light. He also displayed unusual sensitivity and rare character traits, which, when they surfaced, evoked great wonder. People in his vicinity felt that a bright star was making its appearance on the horizon that would shine with a dazzling brilliance for generations to come.

Early Marriage

Before his *bar mitzvah* he was betrothed to the daughter of one of the most distinguished families in Broide, Hinda Rachel. He was married at fourteen and was supported at his father-in-law's table in Valkovisk after his marriage. Throughout this time, he devoted all of his waking hours to Torah study.

During the period of his engagement, Yehoshua Leib became critically ill. Someone close to his father suggested that they annul the betrothal as a *segulah* for his recovery. But before making any such move, R' Binyamin said that he had to consult with his son.

He entered his son's bedroom and asked him about such a *segulah*. R' Yehoshua Leib rejected the idea firmly, saying, "And what should all the sick people do for a *segulah* if they happen not to be *chasanim*?"

A resident of Valkovisk, R' Benzion Sternfeld, praised R' Yehoshua Leib's greatness during his early years, saying, "I can testify that during his stay in Valkovisk, he was already fluent in *Talmud Bavli* with all the commentaries and even knew the entire *Talmud Yerushalmi* by heart."

HIS FATHER RELIED UPON HIM implicitly in every thing, entrusting to him the most complex matters, despite his tender age.

And Then Again

R' Yehoshua Leib related the following incident to R' Aryeh Leib Frumkin:

"My esteemed father once came to me with a *din Torah*, involving two rich men and tens of thousands of rubles. Each litigant was backed by famous rabbis and it was up to my father to be the final arbitrator. This case dragged out for several weeks without coming any closer to a solution. Finally, my father came to me, asking me to take on the case and settle it once and for all.

"I shied away from this task, for the rabbis involved were noted authorities. One of them was a venerable sage of advanced age and great stature. But my father urged me to study the case since he was not in the best of health and it was proving too much of a burden for him. I took the keys to the room containing the documents of the case so that I could inspect them before the *beis din* convened.

"I studied the various arguments — nineteen claims and defenses — and leaned towards one side.

"When the people involved appeared in the court, I stated my opinion, as arbitrator, that one side was justified in its first argument. But the defender of the opposite side, the venerable rabbi, refused to accept my opinion. All of my efforts to convince him were in vain. I repeated myself and clarified my words but he refused to be convinced.

"I had no desire to rule against him without him agreeing with me, for he was a most learned and accepted authority. And so, I let the case rest for the while, saying that we would continue the discussion on the morrow.

"I attacked the case from the fifth point on the following day. This time I admitted that justice lay with the other side, to which the elder sage happily agreed. I then turned about and argued the same point from the opposing view until he finally broke down and admitted that I was right. He conceded my arguments against this fifth point.

"Having scored a victory, I said that I had no wish to contort the law from its straightforward solution. And so, switching sides, I took up this very fifth point from an opposite direction, for I wanted to get to the pure truth. I now upheld *his* position on this point but challenged the first point, showing him how he had been mistaken.

"In the end, he had to admit that I was right in everything."

WHEN HE WAS ABOUT TO turn eighteen, his father informed him, several days in a row, that he wished to impart something very

His Father's Legacy

important and vital to him, and that he should prepare himself for a momentous event.

On R' Yehoshua Leib's eighteenth birthday, his father called him in and said, "My son, you are sanctified from the womb and have acquired the crown of Torah. The time has now come for you to accept the yoke of Heaven in fear and awe. From now on you are to tread a chosen, unique path."

That day forever remained firmly etched in R' Yehoshua Leib's memory, for then, R' Yehoshua Leib chose his unique path in life and formed the guidelines for his future conduct.

His son, R' Yitzchak Yerucham, used to say that he was told that whatever he saw in his great father — his asceticism, dedication, scrupulousness in every detail — began on that day of his eighteenth birthday, when R' Binyamin took him aside and steered him on the path of life.

CHAPTER FOUR

The Rabbinate

R' YEHOSHUA LEIB SOUGHT TO LIVE IN PEACE, secluded in the tent of Torah, studying and teaching. However, Heaven will-

Lomza —
His Father's
Successor

ed otherwise.

The burden of the rabbinate caught up with him when he was a young man of twenty-seven. From the backwaters of Valkovisk, he was suddenly deposited in Lomza, a major center of Jewish learning. His ascent to fame was meteoric, catapulting him from a life of obscurity and isolation to one of leadership on a grand scale.

When the Jews of Lomza lost their great leader, R' Binyamin Diskin, in 5604 (1844), they convened an assembly of all the scholars and communal figures of the city. Unanimously setting their sights upon his firstborn son who had dazzled everyone with his genius and holiness, they decided to offer him his father's position.

A distinguished delegation representing the congregation of Lomza was dispatched to the home of R' Yehoshua Leib's father-in-law with a certificate of appointment signed by the elders of the city.

R' Yehoshua Leib saw this as a sign from Heaven and did not shy

A company of German soldiers march down the main street of Lomza following their take over the city during World War I.

away from the responsibility. He accepted the contract and set a date for his arrival.

The people of Valkovisk were sorry to lose their treasure on the one hand, but were proud that the young man who had graced them with his presence was awarded such a prestigious office. They all flocked to congratulate him and wish him success in his new post.

When the day of departure arrived, R' Yehoshua Leib was transported to Lomza in grand style. All the people of the city, dressed in their holiday attire, waited at the outskirts of the city to greet him, amidst great fanfare. There was a resounding shout as soon as the new rav's coach was first sighted in the distance. All eyes were peeled to catch a glimpse of him.

R' Yehoshua Leib's influence was soon felt in the entire city and outlying areas. His sharp eye surveyed all aspects of communal life, which he administered efficiently and impartially.

The people of Lomza felt that their lives had been infused with a new holiness. If a resident ever happened to visit another city, he was unable to refrain from praising his home town and mentioning his rav's name with awe. The Jews of Lomza gloried in his leadership.

A SHORT WHILE AFTER R' Yehoshua Leib was initiated into office, the townspeople had occasion to fully appreciate the quality of his

The Unfulfilled Threat

leadership. The government had just passed a law obligating every educational institution to teach the language of the land. R' Yehoshua Leib opposed secular studies of any type and he had no intention of allowing any other language to be taught within the walls of the *chadarim* in his city.

One informer went to the governor and revealed that the religious schools were making a sham of the law. The teachers were not teaching the national tongue and students were not able to converse in it.

The governor summoned the heads of the Jewish community and demanded that they explain themselves. They referred him to the rav, as he had the final say on all matters pertaining to education.

The governor summoned R' Yehoshua Leib. Handing him a sheet of paper, the governor demanded that he write out orders to the members of his community to obey the law of the land. He refused.

The governor leapt up in a rage and shouted, "I have urgent affairs to discharge in Warsaw and must leave immediately. I have no time for this matter right now. But, you may be sure that immediately upon my return I will take the necessary measures to force you to write and sign my orders."

But the governor was never able to make good on his threat. As he was leaving the city, the bridge collapsed under his coach and he drowned.

AT THAT TIME, POLAND WAS in the throes of a revolution. R' Yehoshua Leib had to appear before General Ganitzka, a figure who

No Room for Fear

struck terror in the hearts of all. R' Yehoshua Leib's proud stance at this meeting became a byword for Jews and Christians alike. The encounter was vividly described in *Hamodia*:

The saintly R' Yehoshua Leib Diskin, rav of Lomza, received orders to appear with some other prominent figures before General Ganitzka. The general's very name evoked terror. The *gaon* was the only one who received the orders with equanimity. On the morrow, he sat ensconced

The square where the reception for the general took place

in his room, studying as usual. At 8:30 in the morning, he put on his festive clothing and went with his *shammash* to the palace gates where everyone had long since been awaiting the general's arrival.

Gathered there were various delegations, including priests of all denominations. The people stood there petrified with fear. Only the rav remained calm and serene, as if he were patiently waiting for the clouds to disperse so that he could recite the blessing over the new moon.

His complete composure astonished all those present. Later, those close to the rav asked him why he had been so unruffled. He replied: "The commandment 'not to fear from any man' is obligatory upon a person's entire body, all of his organs and sinews. If one controls one's entire body, then there is no room left for fear. My father perfected this mastery over fear until it became natural, a part of his makeup. By me, it is only hereditary."

R' YEHOSHUA LEIB FULFILLED the precept of "You shall not fear before any man" inwardly as well as outwardly. If he had to enforce

The Disappointed Shochet

the law against people close to him, he did not flinch.

When he was first appointed to the rabbinate in Lomza, the long-time *shochet* of the city was a highly esteemed, renowned scholar.

In the course of time, R' Yehoshua Leib discovered that the *shochet* drank heavily and was fearful that this might affect his performance. Against R' Yehoshua Leib's better judgment, he did not immediately suggest that the man be dismissed, since the *shochet* was an expert in his field and highly regarded in the community. Besides, he had served during R' Binyamin's lifetime.

At this time, an opening for the position of *shochet* arose in Plotzk. The Lomza *shochet*'s name was brought up as a candidate, since he enjoyed a fine reputation. The city's elders approved the suggestion and offered him a contract with excellent terms.

The *shochet* took their letter of appointment and went to discuss the matter with R' Yehoshua Leib.

R' Yehoshua Leib was straightforward. "I disapprove," he said.

Weeks passed and the *shochet* received a second invitation from the Plotzk community, which emphasized the excellent terms of the contract. He again went to consult with R' Yehoshua Leib, who reiterated his opposition.

Again, the *shochet* turned down the offer and continued to serve in Lomza. But the Jews of Plotzk did not give up. They selected two delegates to go to Lomza and personally plead with the *shochet* to come, but the *shochet* would not make the decision alone. He went to the rav a third time and told him of the two men who had come to take him to Plotzk.

R' Yehoshua Leib listened and said, "If they have actually come to fetch you and are very insistent, as you say, and if you are willing, I will not stand in the way."

"But," he continued, "if you do decide to leave, I am giving you a six-week leave of absence. I will hold your position open for you for the next six weeks. If you do not return by then, I will appoint another *shochet* in your place and you will have no further claim to your old post."

The *shochet* agreed. He parted and left the city with his two escorts. But, when he arrived in Plotzk, he found the city bitterly divided between his supporters and those of another candidate. Even though, in the beginning, it looked as if the faction favoring the Lomza *shochet* would win, slowly the tide turned against him and his supporters dwindled.

Now he was stuck in Plotzk, waiting with a faint glimmer of hope that he would regain favor. But it was in vain, for his opponent was awarded the position of *shochet*. And meanwhile, the six-week waiting period had already expired.

When the Lomza *shochet* saw that he was defeated, he packed his things and returned to Lomza, expecting to return to his former post. He went to R' Yehoshua Leib and described the events that had brought him back, expressing his regret that he had ever left Lomza.

R' Yehoshua Leib reminded him that he no longer had any claim to the office in Lomza, either. Bitterly disappointed, he left the rav's house and poured out his troubles to his close acquaintances. They came as a group to beg R' Yehoshua Leib to reconsider his decision and restore the *shochet* to his former job.

R' Yehoshua Leib said to them, "When I came here, I found this man filling the post. I was not the one who hired him; he merely continued to hold what had been his by right of tenure. When he asked me whether to go to Plotzk, I advised him against it. He begged me to allow him to leave and I did so, even giving him a six-week grace period. If he chose to linger on and let the allotted time expire, it is purely his fault. He consciously defaulted and has no claim to the position here. You have come to ask me to hire him anew upon my responsibility, but that I will not do."

That *motzaei Shabbos*, after a *melaveh malkah* meal together, the *shochet*'s friends decided to importune R' Yehoshua Leib once more. A large group reached his house. When he asked what had brought them so late at night, they began defending their colleague. They reminded him that the *shochet* had served the city faithfully for thirty years!

In typical fashion, R' Yehoshua Leib repeated his previous reply verbatim, not omitting or adding a single word. He laid special emphasis on his refusal to appoint him *anew* as a positive act on his part. The people crowding into his room asked him to give a reason. He refused. "I cannot tell you why," he said simply.

When they saw that his mind had been made up, they renewed their efforts with harsh words, crudely demanding that he reinstate the *shochet*. R' Yehoshua Leib grasped onto the armrests of his chair and thundered at them, "Have you come to argue with me?" And he said no more.

The men buried their heads in shame. The leonine roar had put fear into their hearts. They turned about and slunk away.

Nevertheless, the *shochet*'s friends were only momentarily abashed. They regrouped the next day and decided to make one last attempt to help him. They decided to bring the matter to one of the leaders of the generation for arbitration. Setting their sights upon the Gerrer Rebbe, the *Chiddushei HaRim*, they wrote a letter describing the circumstances and waited for his decision.

His reply was not long in coming: "I would not dare oppose the word of the rav of Lomza."

The tempest died down.

The Burdens of the Rabbinate

NO ONE COULD FIND FLAW or fault with his conduct in public matters. Everything bore his seal of approval and administration; everything was subject to his scrutiny. Nothing escaped his sharp eye.

His job entailed both maintaining a strict vigil over the religious affairs of the city and the constant dissemination of Torah. Together, these responsibilities constituted an almost unbearable yoke.

In 5605 (1845), during the first year of his tenure, he already wrote: "I delayed replying until now due to the excessive duties of my office. People surround me all day with practical matters that need attention."

In his responsa we find: "This is what I have fished up in my net with a minimum of research. [I could not devote any more time since] I am heavily burdened with all my affairs. I received your letter a month ago but was so preoccupied that I could not devote any attention to it. I know that this is the third time you have called my attention to it and I cannot turn you away emptyhanded. Now, at midnight, there is no one to disturb me; still, I must be brief."

(Signed) Your preoccupied friend.

IN ADDITION TO THE PUBLIC BURDEN in Lomza which rested on his shoulders, R' Yehoshua Leib was left a widower in Lomza when his

A Young Widower

wife, Hinda Rachel, died. She left one young son, Yitzchak Yerucham, born in 5599 (1839).

R' Yehoshua Leib lavished double care and attention upon his orphan son, educating him in his unique way. This gave him great satisfaction, as he expressed in a letter, "My son studies with me and is very successful, may *Hashem* grant it thus in the future." Indeed, his son grew up to be a brilliant scholar.

Yitzchak Yerucham was still a young lad, under thirteen, when his mother died. The boy was devastated by the loss, and became extremely depressed. During the week of mourning, his father took him aside and told him, "It was a decree from Heaven. I was given the choice of your life or hers and I chose yours. I am certain that were the decision presented to her, she would have chosen the same."

"My father's words had a deep effect upon my soul and succeeded in dissipating my melancholy," R' Yitzchak Yerucham remembered later.

A few years later, R' Yehoshua Leib took a second wife, Sarah (Sonia), the daughter of the esteemed R' Tzvi Hirsh Rotner, and granddaughter of the *Ateres Rosh* and of R' Elazar Landau, author of *Yad Hamelech*. She was also descended from R' Yosef Hatzaddik, *av beis din* of Posen and the son-in-law of the *Noda BeYehudah*.

Rebbetzin Sarah was famous for her intelligence and knowledge, as well as her industriousness and fine character. An unusually righteous woman, she managed the household with all the stringencies and *hiddurim* demanded by her husband and happily abided by the strictest ruling to be found in the *Shulchan Aruch*. She lent her helping hand to every worthy endeavor and secretly supported entire households. She invested great energy, even in her old age, in helping establish her husband's great project, the orphanage named after him in Jerusalem. She was an extremely devoted wife to R' Yehoshua Leib to his very last day.

EVEN THE JEWS OF LOMZA, who were themselves famous for their tireless Torah study, marveled at his assiduity, the like of which they

Teacher of Torah

had never beheld! Night and day, they would see him at his studies, never resting.

The Jews of Lomza could not fathom his amazing dedication, nor did they cease remarking about it. R' Yerucham Fishel Perlow, author of a commentary on *Sefer Hamitzvos* of R' Saadya Gaon, writes that the scholars of Lomza referred to him as "the *malach* (angel)."

R' Yehoshua Leib established a *yeshivah* in the center of Lomza, which drew the cream of gifted young men from near and far. They longed to hear his insights and absorb his piety. He gave in-depth lectures daily, aside from Sabbath and the eve of festivals. Even on *erev Yom Kippur* he delivered a lecture, which he completed after the fast.

He also taught the laymen a daily *shiur* in *Gemara*. He reduced the *Gemara* to its basics and answered every question with a simplicity which was easily comprehended. The scholars of Lomza flocked to the

The beis midrash in Lomza

beis medrash to witness R' Yehoshua Leib's amazing metamorphosis from *rosh yeshivah* to teacher of basics. They likened it to "And Moshe descended from the mountain to the people."

In additional to his daily lectures, he would closet himself each night in study with the most promising of his disciples for six consecutive hours.

One of these select students described his approach to study:

"During the course of study, he would often sink into deep thought and remain as if in meditation for a long spell. Then, slowly, he would shake himself out of that state and begin murmuring softly to himself, expounding different approaches to the problem and refuting them accordingly. If, after his pondering, he still had not reached a satisfactory solution, he would ask the student to repeat the text of the *Gemara* clearly, word for word. He would then get up and pace the room in deep concentration until a torrent of tears would burst from his eyes. Weeping, he would go off into a corner and pray with a broken heart, 'Answer me, *Hashem*. Favor me. Illuminate my eyes with Your Torah.' He would say *vidui* (confession) and deposit some money in the R' Meir Baal HaNess charity box. Then his eyes would light up. He had emerged from the straits."

This scene repeated itself frequently.

THE CENTER OF HIS ACTIVITY was Lomza, but his influence spread far and wide. The elders of his generation turned to him, even in the

His Fame Spreads early days of his rabbinate, for his guidance and as a mediator. R' Yehoshua Leib replied to all inquiries, but paid special attention to matters of a practical nature.

He devoted much effort to easing the plight of *agunos*, women bound to husbands who had disappeared, and found grounds to permit many such women to remarry.

Soon after he arrived in Lomza, a man mysteriously disappeared and was reported to have been murdered. His wife became an *agunah*. R' Yehoshua Leib's writ of release for the woman amazed the scholars of the generation and drew public attention to him. Soon he was besieged with requests to help in other difficult cases of *agunos*.

A woman whose husband had drowned in the Dnieper River came to plead for permission to remarry. Though initially he found no basis for permitting remarriage, R' Yehoshua Leib would not give up trying to help the unhappy woman. And he succeeded, to the surprise of all the great scholars of Russia, who had been following the story with great interest. The writ of release included fifty-seven different lines of argument.

From his correspondence, we see how many rabbis refused to permit an *agunah* to remarry without his approval, even when he was still in his twenties.

Not a Wasted Word

WHEN HE SPOKE WITH PEOPLE who came to him in person, he limited the exchange to a few words. He never engaged in conversation for its own sake and was in perfect control of his tongue, never uttering an unnecessary word.

R' Naftali Hertz, rav of Jaffa, described him as "never saying a word for which there was not a parallel in the language of *Chazal*."

The questioner would leave R' Yehoshua Leib's home fortified with a definite line to follow, a clear-cut 'No' or 'Yes,' 'Do' or 'Don't.' Sometimes, people did not take his replies seriously enough due to his curtness. They did not realize that in his two or three-word reply, he had grasped all the elements of the question and resolved it in the best possible way. Even the head of the community once made this mistake.

Czar Nicholas I of Russia undertook to build a major highway connecting St. Petersburg to Warsaw. A festive dedication ceremony was planned for its inauguration, with the Czar himself traveling from one end of the highway to the other. Lomza, which was approximately midway on the journey, was chosen as a stopover for the royal entourage.

The Jews of Lomza prepared a royal welcome for the monarch. They decorated the city, cleaned up its streets and scrubbed all the stairs and courtyards which faced the procession route, as if in readiness for a festival. Windows in homes and shops were bedecked with curtains and flags of the national colors. Flowerpots appeared in every window.

As preparations reached a fever pitch, Reb Yisrael Dubinsky, the wealthy president of the community, came to consult the rav concerning preparations for receiving the Czar. In the midst of their conversation, R' Yehoshua Leib suddenly told him, "I would advise you not to appear before the Czar."

Reb Yisrael did not take the warning seriously and promptly forgot all about it. He could not imagine himself, as president of the community, foregoing the honor of being its representative.

The long-awaited day finally arrived. The Czar, together with his military escort, entered Lomza. Reb Yisrael Dubinsky, representing the Jewish community, went forth to greet him and show him the Jewish quarter. He pointed out its landmarks and highlights, singling out the great synagogue and *yeshivos*, the factories, business centers and so on.

In the course of his tour, Reb Yisrael showed the Czar around the Jewish hospital, which he himself had established. It was housed in a magnificent structure and built on a grand scale.

The Czar pointed out a certain fault in the building. In defense, Reb Yisrael argued that the hospital had been constructed according to a famous architect's plan. The Czar continued walking and, a few steps later, pointed out another flaw in the hospital's design. Reb Yisrael again tried to refute the Czar's criticism by explaining the advantages of the building. They continued touring the hospital with the Czar again and again indicating errors in the planning, and Reb Yisrael defending himself and trying to convince the Czar that it had been no mistake but was an intentional feature with a definite purpose.

Finally, Reb Yisrael found himself surrounded by armed guards and led away to prison. He had been unaware that the law stated that whenever the Czar criticized a person, the object of his faultfinding was obliged to concede his error and promise that it would be rectified. Reb Yisrael had been unaware of this rule of royal etiquette and, instead of agreeing with the Czar, had tried to convince him that he, Reb Yisrael, was right.

Only after much pleading with the Czar by the community leaders was Reb Yisrael finally released.

When R' Zelig Karelenstein, one of those close to R' Yehoshua Leib, later asked him how he had known to warn Reb Yisrael against appearing at the reception for the Czar, he replied simply, "I know Reb Yisrael to be a forthright person and imagined that he would make some error and antagonize the Czar in one way or another."

LOMZA. *ELUL* 5619 (1859).

Mezeritch and Kovno

The skies were overcast; the atmosphere tense. In addition to the usual trembling in anticipation of the approaching Days of Judgment, a hidden anxiety lurked in the hearts of the residents.

A distinguished delegation from Mezeritch had been visiting in the city for a week. The emissaries seemed fatigued. They rushed constantly about, whispering secrets, meeting among themselves, as well as with R' Yehoshua Leib in his study. The purpose of their visit was shrouded in secrecy.

The people of Lomza studied their guests with suspicion. What business had brought them to their city? And what affairs kept them closeted so frequently with their rav? Were they about to "steal" their rav away from them?

Many rumors floated about but nothing was clear. In vain did R' Yehoshua Leib's disciples try to extract some information from the venerable R' Zelig Karelenstein.

At last, R' Yehoshua Leib revealed to his beloved disciples and precious townspeople that he was about to leave them. He summoned his followers to his home on the hillside and announced that he had accepted the offer from Mezeritch to be their rav. He was about to leave Lomza.

Morning arrived.

The way to R' Yehoshua Leib's house was packed with people. From early dawn, the city's scholars, elders, businessmen and laymen flocked to the rav's house. By the time the sun rose, the house was encircled with people.

His parting speech was short but deeply emotional. Each person absorbed and interpreted the measured words according to his level of understanding.

The leave-taking completed, R' Yehoshua Leib left his house

dressed in festive attire. His *talmidim* helped him into the waiting coach. A shower of blessings fell from all sides. The coach inched its way through the roadblock of humanity and started rolling down the mountain in the direction of Mezeritch. The people of Lomza, watching the vehicle bearing their rav far away, burst into unabashed tears.

No one dared to bring up the dreaded topic of a replacement. In the eyes of the Lomza community, the rav had not even left. The people refused to admit that he was gone; the rav had merely moved his tent somewhat further away. But he was still their rav; his holy spirit still hovered over the city as before. The people of Lomza consoled themselves with the jest that R' Yehoshua Leib had not left Lomza at all; rather, Lomza had expanded all the way to Mezeritch.

"A stranger shall not occupy his throne." Thus did the elders of Lomza rule when their rav left their midst. His seat in the *beis medrash* stood empty, as if waiting for him to return and occupy it as before.

The people of Lomza waited for their rav to return. And they did not wait in vain.

Mezeritch prepared itself to replace Lomza as a spiritual center. However, it soon became apparent that Mezeritch was not a suitable vessel to hold such a great luminary as R' Yehoshua Leib. Mezeritch enjoyed the privilege of hosting him for only one winter before he moved on to Kovno.

But Kovno, too, failed to provide R' Yehoshua Leib the spiritual fare he needed. The atmosphere was not to his liking and before long, he decided to leave Kovno:

A religious writer of the times summed up R' Yehoshua Leib's sojourn in Kovno:

> He accepted the position in Kovno but did not remain there for long. Its residents were primarily businessmen and many of them had turned astray to follow the *Haskalah*, which already held sway and had lured away many of our worthy Lithuanian brothers. Kovno could not endure his intense holiness and zeal for Torah. And so the people became fractious.

ACTUALLY, HOWEVER, there was an additional factor which brought about R' Yehoshua Leib's departure from Kovno.

A Monopoly Is Broken

In those days, the city would sell the franchise on the meat tax to the highest bidder. Whoever acquired that right would collect the *shechitah* tax for the next three years, but he would be obliged to cover the communal needs.

Communal law required that the trustees hold a public auction for this franchise. Over the years, however, changes crept in. One rich and influential family in Kovno appropriated the franchise for themselves. The members of this family had access to high officials and wielded influence with the government officials. So firmly entrenched was this family that the people of Kovno did not even dream of asserting their rights and did not bother attending the public auction. People who might have been in a position to bid against them were afraid to do so and the procedure became a farce.

The community suffered most from this situation, for the family holding the franchise neglected its communal duties; its contribution to communal projects was negligible and the public felt the brunt of the loss. When R' Yehoshua Leib became the rav in Kovno, the trustees went to him with their problem. They decried the family's hold on the meat tax and complained bitterly about the suffering which it caused the community.

When R' Yehoshua Leib heard this, he rose to his full height and said in a commanding tone: "This shall not continue!"

The day of the public auction approached. R' Yehoshua Leib made it known that he expected to see the entire community at the event. He, too, would grace the auction with his presence. Meanwhile, he spoke with the other wealthy members of the community who were in a position to bid against the incumbent family. He ordered his *shammash* to inform all the members of the congregation that he personally expected everyone to be present.

When the time came, the auditorium was packed, in sharp contrast to previous years. The rav was also there.

The government officials authorized to supervise the bidding went up to the rostrum. The meeting began. The bidding began with a low sum of one hundred rubles. Members in the audience quickly raised it to eight thousand rubles. At this point, the incumbent family shouted that it bid nine thousand rubles.

The large gathering held its breath. This was an unheard-of sum. Any higher bid meant direct confrontation with the family in power, but not to bid further meant disobeying the rav!

The auctioneer was about to wind up the meeting, awarding the tender to the high bidder, when R' Yehoshua Leib broke the silence. He rose to his feet and bid thirty thousand rubles for the *shechitah* franchise.

A rustle swept the crowd. The members of the incumbent family exchanged signals with one another and whispered mockingly at the rav's bid; everyone knew that he was virtually penniless and would never be able to pay his commitment. The officials on the platform also writhed uncomfortably at this sudden jump. They did not know how to react to the rav's outrageous bid.

R' Yehoshua Leib worked his way up to the front and laid three thousand rubles down on the table. The law stipulated that the buyer had to put down ten percent of his bid in cash.

The rav's courage was contagious. But the bidding was not yet over. The head of the incumbent family upped the price to thirty-five thousand rubles. Inspired at the rav's action, other bidders raised the price. The competition was lively and swift, until someone bid seventy thousand rubles and won the franchise.

R' Yehoshua Leib's part in breaking up the monopoly made a tremendous impact upon the city. The public institutions rejoiced that they would now begin receiving many times their former subsidies. Still, the people shivered in anticipation of the defeated family's revenge.

A FEW YEARS EARLIER there had been an uprising against the Czarist government, which had been put down firmly. But here and there,

The Loser's Revenge

pockets of insurgents continued to exist. The defeated family took advantage of this situation by accusing the rav of being a leader of such a rebel group and of supporting it with huge sums of money.

The slander reached the authorities on a Thursday. By the next morning the rav was summoned to appear before the provincial authorities. He was briefly told the charges against him. The law required that he be arrested and brought under armed guard to Vilna, until he was exonerated or punished. The deputy governor explained to R' Yehoshua Leib that since the governor was away and it was already Friday, he would release him upon his word of honor until Sunday morning.

R' Yehoshua Leib turned white when he heard the charges against him, but he composed himself and returned home serenely. It did not take long for the entire city to learn about the false charges. The community seethed with the shocking news. The leaders of the congregation were summoned for an emergency meeting in the rav's house to seek a way to fend off the impending evil.

That Friday, R' Yosef Dov Soloveitchik, the *Beis HaLevi*, arrived in Kovno from Volozhin. Exhausted from the arduous journey, the first thing he did was to pray. Then he went to the home of his father, R' Yitzchak Zev, to rest. At the breakfast table he learned from his father, one of the communal trustees, of the showdown with the dominant family and the rav's role in defying them. At that very moment, the door opened and in rushed the *shammash* of the *beis din*, panting heavily, to notify R' Yitzchak Zev of the emergency meeting which would soon take place in the rav's house.

"What could be so urgent on a Friday morning?" R' Yitzchak Zev asked, still ignorant of the latest developments. When the two men learned of the threat hanging over the rav's head, they both rushed to the rav's house. R' Yosef Dov forgot all about his weariness. As soon as R' Yehoshua Leib beheld his eminent guest, he rose, ran over to him and embraced him fervently.

The official town rabbi, the Kazianer Rav, Rabbi Manischevitz, related how he had visited the chief secretary in the cabinet and thanked him for releasing the rav until Sunday. He had learned that the governor was expected to return late that evening. The participants then began heatedly discussing what to do next. Some insisted that a delegation of three prominent men should visit the governor the next day and beg him to revoke the charges. Others were of the opinion that this was futile, since the case was to be heard in Vilna, where the governor did not wield much influence. They were convinced that a delegation should be sent to Vilna, to intercede directly with the governor there, especially since he was known to accept bribes.

R' Yosef Dov sat deep in thought, murmuring something unintelligible. R' Yehoshua Leib turned to him and asked, "And what can the Volozhiner *Rosh Yeshivah* add?"

"With the rav's permission and the permission of my honored father," he began, "I would like to offer my opinion, even though I am no more than a guest in your midst. I maintain that one must put pressure upon the local governor, but not through a delegation of three men. I think that the entire city should stage a demonstration of sympathy."

The participants stared at R' Yosef Dov in wonder. What did he mean?

"Actually," he continued, "my plan is not easy to carry out. But, if you agree to follow my instructions for as long as I am here, I trust, with the help of the Almighty, that all will turn out right."

All eyes turned to the rav to see his reaction. After a brief pause, he said, "We can all rely on R' Yosef Dov and rest assured that Hashem will favor any course he suggests."

R' Yosef Dov summoned the *gabbaim* of all the *batei medrash* in the city and told them that on *Shabbos* morning there was to be only one *minyan*. The *gabbaim* were to stand by the doors of their respective synagogues and direct all the people who came to pray toward the main synagogue.

The scene that took place in Kovno that *Shabbos* morning was never to be repeated. Jews from all the corners of the city streamed towards the central synagogue. Within a short time, thousands had assembled. This huge procession began moving towards the governor's mansion, led by the official rabbi, the Kazianer Rav, who was flanked by the president and the trustees of the community.

When the police beheld the size of the crowd, they ran to fetch reinforcements, thinking that the Jews were staging a rebellion. Soon a large force was making its way towards the mass of people.

When the police saw that the procession was being led by the chief rabbi and two of the community leaders, they sheathed their drawn weapons. The chief of police ordered his men to escort the dignitaries to the governor's mansion to make sure that order was maintained. He, meanwhile, sped ahead to notify the governor of the huge crowd which was making its way towards him.

The governor's chief secretary was already waiting to receive the delegation. He requested the reason for this huge gathering. The Kazianer Rav stepped forward and said, "The entire Jewish community of Kovno is deeply disturbed by the false charges made against our beloved rav, whom we all know to be a pure and holy man. He is true to his country and loyal to its laws. We have come here to beg the governor to withdraw the charges against him and we are resolved to wait here peaceably until we hear an announcement to that effect."

The secretary asked the delegation to wait while he took the matter up with the governor. Meanwhile, the people began reciting *Tehillim*. R' Yosef Dov recited the psalms verse by verse, while the immense crowd repeated after him. After a few chapters, he began the fifteen *Shir Hamaalos*. When he came to the words, "*Hashem*, save my soul from the lips of falsehood, from the tongue of deception," he uttered them in a heartbreaking tone. Everyone burst into tears. R' Yosef Dov continued reciting and as soon as he came to the words, "*Hashem* did mightily with us; we rejoiced," the secretary reappeared on the balcony waving a sheet of paper. He asked for the public's and attention in an instant, everyone was still. Silence reigned, as all craned their necks to see what would occur next.

"His Excellency, the Governor Nikolai Maravyov, requests the pardon of his loyal subjects for not coming out to address them in person, as he is ill. But he asked me to say in his name that he will never forget the moving scene which took place half a year ago when the Jews of Kovno prayed for the welfare of their new Czar, Alexander II, upon his coronation, and when the rav of Kovno opened the Holy Ark and kissed the Torah scrolls. He looked like a veritable angel on that memorable occasion. The governor says that he cannot possibly conceive that such a holy man would have anything to do with insurgents. He regards the accusations as evil slander and declares the rav to be completely exonerated of participation in any plot against the Czar."

His words were hailed with great joy. Then the crowd dispersed and people went off to their respective synagogues to say the morning prayers and to thank Hashem for His speedy succor.

A few days later, the governor's secretary appeared in the rav's house to inform him that the family from which he had wrested the slaughter-tax franchise was still bent on revenge. This time they planned to strike in such a way that even the governor would be helpless to intervene since it would involve higher powers. He advised the rav to leave Kovno for some time until matters died down.

R' Yehoshua Leib discussed the issue with R' Yosef Dov. Despite the fact that R' Yehoshua Leib was not one to be intimidated, the two Torah giants decided that in this case, it was wiser to be on the safe side and not antagonize the enemy when lives were possibly at stake. It was therefore decided that R' Yehoshua Leib leave Kovno. He was replaced by the former Novardhok rav, R' Yitzchak Elchanan Spector, a childhood friend of R' Yehoshua Leib and a disciple of his father.

A REMARKABLE STORY concerning R' Yehoshua Leib during his time in Kovno was told by R' Zorach Braverman, who heard it from R' Yehoshua Leib himself.

The Recurring Dream

A poor man, who supported his family by selling produce in the marketplace, had a strange dream. At first he ignored it, but it recurred two times. He dreamed that he saw his father, who had passed away that very year. His father urged him to go to a certain village, to a certain house and to offer to buy a black bull from the gentile farmer living there. The farmer, he was told, would ask for eighty rubles, but would settle for half the amount. The son was to take this bull and slaughter it in Kovno and distribute its meat to the poor. This act would be the father's *tikkun*; it would release his soul, which had entered the bull, and enable it to enter *Gan Eden*.

The poor man, whose earnings of two or three rubles a week barely sufficed to feed his family, did not know what to make of the dream. One day, he was leading the prayers when, suddenly, he fainted. When he was revived, he told the people that he had seen a vision of his father, again, for the fourth time. They took him to R' Yehoshua Leib to see what should be done.

The rav listened carefully. Then he turned to the people standing about and asked, "The bull must be redeemed. But who shall pay for it? And who shall pay for the time that this Jew loses in going to fetch it?" A few people spoke up and offered to cover the costs. The rav then turned to the man and said, "Go and do exactly as your father instructed you in the dream. But do not buy the black bull unless all the conditions are met. The village must be the one he described. The house must be identical, the price right, and so on." The man went and found that everything tallied exactly with his dream. He bargained the gentile down to forty rubles and went to the barn to claim his purchase. "You will need help in leading it home," said the farmer, "since it is a wild, unruly beast." The Jew ignored his words. He tied a rope around the beast's neck and it was as docile as a lamb.

The Jew led it to Kovno and brought to the slaughterhouse. R' Yehoshua Leib was present when the animal was slaughtered and responded *amen* to the *shochet*'s blessing. The animal proved to be kosher upon inspection and its meat was distributed among the poor scholars of the city. A portion was also sent to the rav, who ate of it.

R' YEHOSHUA LEIB LEFT KOVNO. As soon as the people of Lomza heard that he was without a position, they begged him to return. They

Return to Lomza

longed for those golden days when he had been their shepherd. When he visited Lomza to see his mother and to pray at his father's grave, the people seized the opportunity to present him with a contract, which they had speedily drawn up for him.

R' Yehoshua Leib's heart softened towards his flock. He accepted the writ of *rabbanus* and told them that he would remain in their midst.

The Lomza community was beside itself with joy. The happy news was borne as if upon waves and reached all the corners of the city. Everyone was thrilled to welcome him back to their midst. The city of Lomza was "widowed" no longer.

He found what he was looking for in Lomza. He bore a special love for its residents, who obeyed his teachings to the letter. The bastion of Judaism was firm and fortified in Lomza; everything was in perfect order and under the rav's total discipline.

BUT THE CITY OF SHKLOV lacked a leader.

Shklov Its rabbinate had been vacant for some time, with no candidate in sight. The vacancy was not due to any dearth of scholars and rabbis in Shklov. On the contrary, Shklov boasted a wealth of learned, pious men. In fact, it supplied rabbis and spiritual leaders for the cities and communities in its vicinity.

There was another reason for the vacancy in Shklov. The scholars of Shklov were determined to have R' Yehoshua Leib as their leader. The city saw itself as deserving of the crown of Diaspora Jewry.

The people of Shklov knew that the Jews of Lomza would not easily relinquish their great prize and would guard their rav with all their might and not let anyone take him away. They remembered well the tearful scene that had taken place when R' Yehoshua Leib had left Lomza for Mezeritch. But Shklov was willing to wait.

The communities all about Shklov wondered and asked: Were they not obsessed by a delusion which would end in grave disappointment? Was it not mad to wait so long in the vain hope that the rav of Lomza would come to serve them?

And yet, the scholars of Shklov asserted confidently that if Mezeritch had been fortunate, and Kovno in its turn, then why not Shklov? Was this city not comparable to the "*mizrach* wall" of all Russian and Lithuanian communities? It was the first and foremost of Jewish centers in both scholarship and numbers, in Torah study and Torah dissemination. Why should it not aspire to acquire the diadem of the Diaspora to crown its glory?

The sages of Shklov traveled through the huge Russian and Lithuanian landscape, visiting great and esteemed communities, pleading with them to stand by Shklov, to put in a good word for it with the rav of Lomza and persuade him to move to their city. The cleverness of the emissaries of Shklov stood them in good stead. They painted a bleak picture of their situation, which melted the hearts of their listeners. They made all of Eastern Europe partners in their tireless quest.

Having successfully enlisted the sympathy and support of the communities in Russia and Lithuania to their cause, they finally reaped the fruits of their labor.

A deluge of letters from rabbis, community leaders and *roshei yeshivah* from all over the land descended upon R' Yehoshua Leib's house. Letters of recommendation, certificates of approbation on behalf of Shklov and its fine residents, praises of its excellence in Torah study and piety all added to the monumental effort.

The people of Lomza were highly attuned to the undercurrents being stirred by the congregation of Shklov. They knew that it had its eye focused on their rav, but they felt helpless. They had been unable to prevent R' Yehoshua Leib from going to Mezeritch and now, surely, could not hold him back from moving to Shklov.

Still, they held frequent council and desperately spoke about what could be done to hold on to their treasure.

But the battle was not evenly matched.

Lomza's counterattack was silenced when R' Yehoshua Leib revealed that he had made up his mind to leave and serve in Shklov. At this point, the people of Lomza realized that any further urging was futile. Their sentence was sealed, whether they accepted it or not. Shklov had won.

In 5629 (1869) R' Yehoshua Leib took up his post as rav in Shklov.

R' Yehoshua Leib's *yeshivah* was held in great esteem in Shklov. Its enrollment increased constantly. (One of his most famous disciples was R' Yosef Rosen of Rogatchov, the Rogatchover Gaon.) R' Yehoshua Leib treated his disciples with deference and initiated them into his unique approach of study.

The Jews of Shklov saw the rav's powerful hand when it came to matters of religious practice. R' Yehoshua Leib once instructed one of the *shochtim* not to touch an animal unless another *shochet* was standing by. Later, he learned that the *shochet* had not heeded the injunction.

That *Shabbos*, he ordered all of the synagogues to be locked and all the Jews to come to the central *shul*. An immense crowd filled the hall.

No one knew what this commotion was all about, until the reading of the Torah, when R' Yehoshua Leib strode up to the *bimah* enveloped in his *tallis* and announced that he forbade the *shechitah* of that particular *shochet*.

R' YEHOSHUA LEIB SERVED in Shklov until 5633 (1873), when he was asked to take the prestigious post as rav of Brisk.

Brisk For a hundreds of years, Brisk reigned supreme as the unchallenged, prestigious fortress of Torah of Russian Jewry.

If the community of Brisk was sovereign, then it followed that the post as rav of the city was the highest rabbinical post in the land. The position had been held over the centuries by such luminaries as the Maharshal, the Bach and many other illustrious figures. They had imbued the city with its unique stamp of excellence and made it foremost in all of the Diaspora.

However, the time came when Brisk was overshadowed, because the leader of the generation, R' Yehoshua Leib, was serving elsewhere. By virtue of that fact alone, Brisk ceded its primary position.

The elders of Brisk were determined to ensconce R' Yehoshua Leib in their midst. And when they did, they considered the event a historic

The shul in Brisk

triumph. The crown of Brisk had been restored to its rightful place.

Brisk, R' Yehoshua Leib's last position in the Diaspora, was also the peak of his greatness in several aspects. To his joy, he found Brisk to be vibrant and healthy, bursting with Torah and good deeds. It was a flourishing community and well fortified spiritually against outside influences, impervious to the ravages of the *Haskalah*.

During R' Yehoshua Leib's tenure in Brisk, the community rose ever higher. The very name "Brisk" became synonymous with pure Torah and sanctity, and the scholars of the generation used to utter the name Brisk with reverence and awe.

The people of Brisk accorded R' Yehoshua Leib royal honor. Every word that left his lips was living Torah. His rulings, teachings and customs served them as a beacon and guide. Sometimes a mere nod or word became the object of lively discussion and extensive interpretation: "The rav hinted at this, implied that . . ." The scholars of Brisk knew that everything that left his mouth was untainted Torah and therefore worthy of interpretation and intense study.

In Brisk, already so well buttressed in the spiritual sense, R' Yehoshua Leib still found room for improvement. One of the well-known regulations which he instituted was that the members of the local burial society were forbidden to collect a fee from the heirs. Instead, they received their pay from the trustees responsible for the cemetery. This was twenty percent of the fee collected for the plot itself and determined according to the deceased's means and station. The members of the *chevrah kadisha* were not permitted to haggle over the price once the trustees had arrived on a specific sum with the heirs.

R' Yehoshua Leib also abolished another widespread practice. At that time, if a Jew was required to give an oath in a government court, the authorities would make him swear with a Torah scroll in his arms. Each time a Jew appeared in court, the clerks had to fetch a scroll from the nearest synagogue and then return it. This happened time after time and irked R' Yehoshua Leib for he regarded it as a disgrace to the Torah.

One day, he declared that the scrolls could no longer be removed for the purposes of secular oaths. Soon afterwards, a Jew had to appear in court and was required to swear. The court clerks went to fetch the scroll, as usual, but were confronted with the new regulation: the rav had forbidden the removal of the scrolls. The clerks returned empty-handed and informed the judge of the rav's new ruling.

R' Yehoshua Leib was summoned to court and the judge asked him, "Is it true that you have forbidden the scrolls to be brought to court?"

"Yes, the Torah scroll is too precious an item to be carried about so freely. For its sake, the blood of myriads of our people has been spilled; they were tortured, burnt at the stake, murdered and massacred. Hundreds of thousands of our people were sacrificed for the sake of each letter."

The moving explanation, said with such fervor, convinced the judge. He rose from his chair and ceremoniously promised to abolish the practice.

R' Yehoshua Leib's presence and his bearing so impressed the judge that he announced that he was transferring the case to R' Yehoshua Leib's court. From then on that judge would frequently refer complex cases to him.

THREE YEARS PASSED since R' Yehoshua Leib's installation when a tragic incident occurred which would permanently separate him from

R' Yehoshua Leib in Jail

the city.

In 5636 (1876), one of the prominent men of Minsk became a *meshumad*, a convert to Christianity. His wife and her father, an esteemed scholar, tried to coax him into giving her a divorce, but he refused. Her efforts were in vain, as were the pleadings of her family.

Finally, however, he gave in to the pressure. He agreed to divorce her for the sum of 1,800 rubles. The unfortunate woman was a relation of R' Yehoshua Leib's wife and she turned to her for help. The *rebbetzin* undertook the project of raising the enormous sum, but only succeeded in gathering 1,400 rubles.

Without telling the *rebbetzin*, the wife went to her estranged husband and told him that the entire sum had already been placed with the rav, pending the divorce. She probably relied on the fact that the entire sum would be raised in time.

The apostate believed her, especially since she said that the sum was in the rav's possession, and that he had arranged for the divorce. As the final date for the giving of the divorce drew near, people warned the woman that if she did not obtain the entire sum, the apostate, who was known to be a vengeful, volatile person, might take some drastic action. Having failed to produce the missing amount and having no recourse, the *askanim* involved spread the rumor that four hundred rubles had been stolen from the rav's home. In order to make their story more plausible, they also notified the police of the "theft." The police opened up an investigation and arrested some likely suspects.

Amidst the police inquiry and arrests, the apostate divorced his wife, believing that his money would be returned to him in time. He was satisfied with having the lion's share and left Brisk for Lublin on business. The *rebbetzin* heaved a sigh of relief when she heard that he had left town. She was already weary of the exhausting searches and endless questions. She told the police that as far as she was concerned, she waived all claim to the "stolen" money.

The police were happy to wash their hands of this affair and closed the case. Slowly, the matter of the "robbery in the rav's house" died down and was forgotten.

The apostate spent some time with a group of priests in Lublin and told them what had happened, proudly flaunting the large sum of 1,400 rubles which he had extorted from his former wife. He also mentioned the four hundred rubles which had been stolen from the rav's house and was still due.

His companions suggested that the theft was only a clever ruse to get him to grant the divorce for 1,400 hundred rubles. The apostate thought it over and became convinced of the truth of what his friends told him. It began to poison his thoughts and gnaw away at him. Obsessed with hatred and thoughts of revenge, he decided to return to Brisk to demand the missing money.

Upon arrival, he went immediately to the *rebbetzin*. When she sent him away, he filed a claim against R' Yehoshua Leib with the police based on two counts: the divorce had been coerced from him against his will and the police had been duped. He substantiated the second claim by the fact that it had been the *rebbetzin* herself who had first notified the police of the theft and it was she who had later withdrawn her pleas and asked them to halt the investigation.

Less than a day later, a police carriage stopped at R' Yehoshua Leib's house and a pair of officials informed the rav that he was under arrest and was to be taken to the prison in Horodna. At the rav's perplexed look, one officer read the official arrest warrant enumerating the two charges against him, for which he would have to be imprisoned pending his trial.

R' Yehoshua Leib raised himself slowly from his seat, wound his special belt around his waist and recited the blessing *Baruch Dayan Emes* — Blessed is the True Judge.

The news spread in a flash and the rav's disciples and family gathered around him. He parted from them with amazing serenity and strode through the parted crowd that had already formed until he reached the vehicle waiting to drive him to prison.

As he was about to climb in, he noticed that the seat inside was upholstered with a mixture of linen and wool, *shaatnez*, and refused to enter. The officers had to bring a different carriage before he agreed to go with them.

R' Yehoshua Leib passed through Bialystock on his way to Horodna. Throngs of townspeople, headed by R' Meir Simcha (author of *Ohr Somayach*), rushed out to escort him. R' Meir Simcha, a happy person by nature, tried to approach and wish the rav a speedy release but drew back. He strode forward a few steps, but could not advance. He later explained that he had felt at that moment that "R' Yehoshua Leib was more in Heaven than on earth."

R' Yehoshua Leib's coach rolled out of Bialystock, leaving the people stunned. They rushed to fill the synagogues with their prayers and lamentations. He was brought to Horodna and cast into a prison cell and shackled alongside thieves and criminals. The gate clanged shut behind him, sealing him from all contact with the outside world. No visitors were allowed.

An oppressive gloom fell on Eastern European Jewry. The leaders of the generation were beside themselves with agony and anxiety, and their fear infected the masses.

A group of distinguished rabbis put aside all other responsibilities in order to obtain a reprieve for the Brisker Rav. They labored day and night to free him from his cell and improve his conditions. Among the Torah giants involved in the efforts on his behalf were R' Yosef Dov Soloveitchik, R' Elya Chaim Meisel, R' Meir Simcha, R' Nachum of Horodna, R' Avraham Shmuel Diskin, his brother, and R' Yitzchak Yerucham, his son.

R' Yosef Dov Soloveitchik

R' Meir Simchah HaKohen of Dvinsk

R' Nachum of Horodna

R' Yitzchok Yerucham Diskin

After several days of round-the-clock exertions, the rabbis realized that there was no chance of freeing R' Yehoshua Leib without a trial. They could not even hope to have him released on bail. Their final hope was to send a special emissary to St. Petersburg. R' Yitzchak Yerucham even traveled on *Shabbos*, but his mission was fruitless.

But the rabbis were not altogether disheartened. They utilized every channel of influence, every possible measure, to save their master. The ceaseless entreaties finally succeeded in gaining preferred treatment for R' Yehoshua Leib. He was to be transferred to a separate cell and permitted visitors. The trial was set for *erev Yom Kippur*.

That day, the iron gate creaked open to admit a group of rabbis who had come to inform him of the good news. Several wardens drew near to remove his handcuffs and lead him to a different cell on the top floor. But R' Yehoshua Leib demurred. When asked why he refused to leave, he said, "There are other Jewish prisoners here, too. Why should I be more privileged than they? Why doesn't anyone intercede for them?" When the rabbis replied that he was innocent whereas they had committed crimes, he replied, "And how do you know? Were you there at the time? How can you positively state that they are guilty if nothing has been proved?"

The rabbis did not bother to reply. They forcibly removed the irons and bore him to the cell which had been prepared for him.

Now that visits were permitted, the prison teemed with people. A *minyan* was established in his cell and a set of Talmud brought for him. From time to time, he was permitted to leave the cell to meet with the other Jewish prisoners. His faith instilled them with new hope and his words revealed new paths of thought.

R' Yehoshua Leib showed amazing agility in removing all *shaat-nez* from the clothing of the Jewish prisoners, pulling it out strand by strand with his own hands. He worked at this until the day of his release. R' Yitzchak Yerucham remarked that hats with *shaat-nez* deserved attention first since they were put on more frequently than clothing and each time they were put on was a separate violation. R' Yehoshua Leib derived special pleasure from this insight.

Elul arrived. People were laboring feverishly to prepare the defense for R' Yehoshua Leib's impending trial. But he was preparing himself for the commandment of blowing the *shofar*. He put all of his heart and soul into fulfilling this particular *mitzvah*, inviting many expert *shofar*-blowers to his cell and winnowing the lot until he settled upon the best.

Rosh Hashanah passed. R' Yehoshua Leib's trial was approaching. The rabbis worked vigorously. There was an air of great activity at all times. A well-known lawyer was hired to represent R' Yehoshua Leib.

The lawyer visited his client two days before the trial to consult with him about the defense. To his surprise, R' Yehoshua Leib turned his head to the wall and refused to look at him.

"What is the meaning of this?" the lawyer asked.

"It is forbidden to gaze upon the face of a wicked man," R' Yehoshua Leib explained.

The lawyer was stunned. When he recovered from the shock, he spoke to R' Yehoshua Leib and tried to convince him to declare before the judges that he had found the money some time after having declared it stolen. But R' Yehoshua Leib would not hear of it. It was not true and he refused to declare a falsehood.

Erev Yom Kippur was fast approaching. Jews throughout Europe again gathered for mass prayers in response to a call from leaders in all the communities. The tension gripped everyone, laymen and scholars alike.

On the afternoon of the trial, the courtroom was filled to bursting, with throngs milling about outside. At the appointed time the judges entered the hall. R' Yehoshua Leib was already seated, waiting. The judges studied him with open curiosity; how grand and regal he looked, how serene and self-contained.

The defense attorney dwelt upon R' Yehoshua Leib's stature and personality, portraying him as a figure before whom all the leaders of Diaspora Jewry bowed in submission and reverence. He even remarked in passing that R' Yehoshua Leib had refused to look him in the face.

This particular fact visibly stirred the judges. They retired to their chambers to reach a decision, but soon sent word that they would announce the sentence only that evening at the time of *Kol Nidrei*.

The courtroom filled again a few hours later. The judge read the sentence in modulated tones: R' Yehoshua Leib was completely exonerated.

An eyewitness later described the scene:

> The trial began on *erev Yom Kippur* at one o'clock in the afternoon. Hundreds of Jews filled the courtroom, standing packed together to hear the mellifluous phrases of the gifted defense lawyer. He swept aside all the accusations of the prosecution. When he finished, the judges retired to a council room and sent word that they would read the sentence at eight o'clock that evening. The Jews then went to the synagogue to imbue the words of the prayer with double meaning: 'Silence the prosecution and lead the defender forth from his place. And may Hashem be his support, for the judgment is Hashem's."
>
> The courtroom was again filled at eight in the evening with our fellow brethren. Their eyes were glued to the door of the judicial chamber where the judges were still sitting in council. Suddenly, they emerged and read out the sentence in his favor. A feeling of relief was felt by all.
>
> How glorious was the sight of R' Yehoshua Leib leaving the prison. The entire street opposite the square of the prison teemed with people waiting to see him. Suddenly, the gate swung open. An elderly man in rabbinical garb emerged, his face inspiring great reverence. He leaned upon the arms of two distinguished men, who had brought him a change of clothing and had come to escort him home. The tremendous crowd followed behind all the way to his home.

On the day following *Yom Kippur* everyone already knew of his release. The news spread to the furthest corners of the Diaspora and evoked great rejoicing.

But it was still feared that any further inquiry into the case would entangle the rav anew and R' Yehoshua Leib was therefore advised to leave Russia altogether.

R' Yehoshua Leib resolved to go up to the Holy Land. On *Chol Hamoed Succos* of 5637 (1877), R' Yehoshua Leib and his *rebbetzin* slipped across the Russian border. They were accompanied by R' Chaim Simcha Soloveitchik, brother of the *Beis HaLevi*. Eventually, they reached France and settled temporarily in Paris.

CHAPTER FIVE

Leader of Jerusalem

I N THOSE DAYS, who dared ascend the Mount of Hashem in Jerusalem? Who dreamed of leaving his country and birthplace, his city and family, to settle on the desolate slopes of Mount Zion? Who contemplated migrating from Europe to wander eastward and set up his tent in the gloomy lanes of a ruined city?

Jerusalem of Yore

Jerusalem of yore was only for people with noble souls who had resolved to renounce commonplace lives and the comforts of civilization. It was for people who had "liquidated" their worldly affairs and saw their future in terms of labor in Torah and purification of their bodies and souls, people who were lovesick and thirsty for G-d and His Divine inspiration, people in whose breasts burned a fierce longing and desire to dwell in the House of Hashem for the remainder of their days.

A visitor from abroad, seeking to understand Jerusalem's holiness, needed only to spend one night within the city's walls. A short while after *Maariv*, the gates of the houses of study would be flung wide

One of the many narrow winding streets of the old city of Jerusalem, c. 1900

open. For the inhabitants of Jerusalem, the Torah they studied by day did not suffice. They were not satisfied with rising at dawn. If the Torah required a Jew to "delve into it by day and by night," that is what they did.

This was the Jerusalem of the World to Come that one entered by invitation only. At midnight, one could see through the cracks in dwellings, the faint glimmer of candles or oil lamps, as Jerusalem's more exalted residents would rise to commiserate with the *Shechinah* in exile.

An air of gloom would descend upon the ruined city. A soft wailing, like the cooing of a mournful dove, could be heard for long stretches throughout the Jewish quarter. It seemed to declare, "Your holy cities became wilderness, O Zion; Jerusalem became a desolate desert."

And in the houses of worship and study, the sound of Torah never ceased. Only the nightwatches changed, one making way for another. The prayer of Jerusalem's Kabbalists with their intense *kavanos* created a special imprint. They prayed according to the Ari Hakadosh's special text, in secluded corners hidden from passersby.

Such was the nightly scene of the "heavenly" Jerusalem.

Even the common people excelled in every aspect of Torah: caution in speech and purity of *middos*, boundless love for Torah, a unique meticulousness in performing every commandment, loyalty to every custom, no matter how strict — all these characterized Jerusalem's dwellers.

The masses of Jerusalem, be they scholars or laymen, craftsmen or shopkeepers, all sent their children to *chadarim*. Parents did not train children for a profession or providing a means of livelihood. Boys were not expected — except in cases of abject poverty — to quit their studies and contribute to the upkeep of the family. These sons were consecrated from conception for Torah study.

People who thought only of their financial security found no home in Jerusalem. The average Jerusalemite lacked the conception of *olam hazeh* — the pleasures of this world. Jerusalem's youth were raised on abstinence. Parents and children sustained themselves with bread dipped in sesame oil or vegetable soup. Jerusalemites looked askance at any effort to better one's economic situation or to improve the norms of nutrition. As precise as they were in speech, as measured in every step and act, so were Jerusalemites orthodox in their habits of eating and drinking, and they loathed any changes for the better.

Despite their poverty and destitution, their faces glowed. They did not see themselves as underprivileged or lacking anything in the Creator's great wide world.

One who never saw Jerusalem during the festivals, in its hour of sublime exaltation, never fully experienced the joy of a *mitzvah*.

One who never felt the elevated atmosphere of Jerusalem in the month of *Elul*, during *Selichos* or the Ten Days of Repentance, when the awe of the Days of Judgment reigned supreme upon all the inhabitants — when even its craftsmen, artisans, smiths and shopkeepers buried themselves in the *Gates of Repentance* of Rabbeinu Yonah — did not know the true meaning of those days.

Every harsh decree or disaster that afflicted any of the tribes of Israel in the Diaspora affected Jerusalem. Her ears were attuned to every cry of pain, every sigh emitted by her sons abroad. She was always alert and ready for prayer and weeping. And when the news arrived that some distant community was beset with woes or that some despot had arisen to trample upon G-d's suffering people, then Jerusalem would proclaim a public prayer assembly and her synagogues would fill with flocks of people. The *shofar* would be blown in Zion and all the *cheder* children would gather in one place and cry out mightily to Hashem to revoke the harsh decree.

The people of Jerusalem divided among themselves the various types of *chessed*. Some supported the destitute, while others ministered to the dead. Still others labored to gladden needy brides or assist widows and orphans, of which the city unfortunately had many. All this was done with no expectation of remuneration.

JERUSALEM — THE SUMMER OF 5637 (1877).

A letter from a Jew in Paris to a relative in Jerusalem threw

R' Yehoshua Leib Arrives

Jerusalem into a state of ecstasy. R' Yehoshua Leib Diskin, who had left his position as the Rav of Brisk and was residing in Paris, was planning to settle in Jerusalem. The news set the city afire. Faces beamed with joy; hearts were swept up in waves of exultation, the likes of which Jerusalem could not recall.

Jerusalemites were so excited that they could hardly believe their ears. Did the leader of the generation really intend to dwell in their midst? Scoffers were not lacking.

Throughout the summer, Jerusalem was in a heightened state of expectation. The sages of Jerusalem conversed about the greatness of the Brisker Rav. Some dwelt upon his brilliance in Torah. Others spoke of his life with awe and wonder. The single theme of all this talk was a fierce yearning for his speedy arrival.

The great day finally arrived. While the menfolk were getting ready to leave the city and greet the Brisker Rav, the women of Jerusalem were also doing their part. They were busy sewing the unique Yerushalmi garment, the gold-striped caftan, which R' Yehoshua Leib had requested and would don even before he entered the city, thus discarding the clothing of the Diaspora.

JERUSALEM, *ROSH CHODESH Menachem Av*, 5637 (1877).

Guardian of the Children

In an unprecedented display of honor, R' Meir Auerbach, former *av beis din* of Kalish and R' Shmuel Salant, the rav of Jerusalem, left the city to greet R' Yehoshua Leib. They were followed by a massive procession of thousands of Jerusalemites.

A roar sprang up from the masses when they first beheld the pride of the generation. The leaders of the community presented him with a writ of *rabbanus* and begged him to accept.

But he did not have his eye on the rabbinate and he ignored the document being extended to him. He had no intention of assuming the yoke of office and managing the numerous affairs of the city. R' Yehoshua Leib's gaze fell upon the little children who were passing before him like so many lambs. His eyes swept over them and feasted upon the heartwarming sight. He was determined to be the guardian of Jewish education.

He never did become the official rav of Jerusalem, nor did he ever accept any specific communal re-

R' Shmuel Salant

sponsibility. From the day of his arrival, however, all the spiritual affairs of the holy city seemed to fall into his able hands. His influence encompassed both the individual and the public.

R' Yehoshua Leib preferred to remain apart from the rabbinical framework. He chose, rather, to protect the holy city and its spiritual assets from without. *To what can this be compared? To an orchard watchman. If he guards it from the outside, it is well guarded. If from within, what lies before him is guarded but what is behind him remains exposed* (Yevamos 21).

He taught the Jerusalem public that only one community existed: the Torah-observant community. Any part of the community which shook off the yoke of the Torah and the *Shulchan Aruch* or uprooted any custom or tradition was to be regarded as an insignificant fringe element of rebels. In his opinion, no official standing could be given such people.

He concentrated all of his efforts upon this theme. Thanks to him, the city was purified of every anti-religious element. The supreme authority in his day was the Torah and the *Shulchan Aruch*. Any public faction which did not abide by them simply did not exist in his time.

That is not to say that there were no individual freethinkers.

There were those who sought to subvert the traditional way of life and establish secular schools. But R' Yehoshua Leib succeeded in having them totally ostracized, banished beyond the "limits of the Israelite camp." They were denied all rights to express their opinion in public matters or municipal affairs.

R' Yehoshua Leib had to be constantly on guard. He could not relax his vigil for even a day nor could he ever rest assured that his work was completed. He was not satisfied to gain independence for Jerusalem's Torah-true Jewry; he fought to assure its sovereignty.

Who else, in an era seething with spiritual turmoil, involving every aspect of Jewish religion and tradition, could have scored so many victories? The *maskilim* in Europe had their sights on the holy city, which depended upon outside support for its existence.

CHAPTER SIX

The Battle Against
Secular Schools

OON AFTER THE REFORM movement raised its ugly head in Hungary and Germany, there sprang up the movement of *Haskalah* and assimilation in Russia, spreading far and wide over vast stretches and threatening the foundations of Jewry. The movement was headed by assimilated Jews. They attempted to "improve" the level of religion and of Jewish education by instituting reforms in Jewish customs. They founded a society called "Promoters of Light and Enlightenment," which established branches in major cities such as Vilna, Kovno, Minsk and Kiev. The society received government accreditation, thanks to the connections of its leaders at court and in the government.

In 5615 (1855) the walls of Jerusalem shuddered when Ludwig Frankel, a representative of the *maskilim* in Europe, established the Lemel school in Jerusalem. The rabbis of Jerusalem immediately issued a ban against the school, but this proved to be only the opening salvo in an ongoing battle.

The Yishuv was then comparatively small and exposed to every wind. It needed a strong captain with courage, who could stand in the breach and confront the Torah's enemies head-on.

Initially, the secularists were few in number, and without powerful contacts abroad. They fully realized that their place was not in the Holy City and that a battle of the spirit was futile. However, in time they began to draw powerful financial support from abroad. Now the battle had to be fought abroad, as well as locally.

In Jerusalem, as well as abroad, all acknowledged that R' Yehoshua Leib was the only one in the generation suited to take on the challenge. Elderly and frail as he was, R' Yehoshua Leib did not hesitate to accept the mantle of leadership.

In the midst of the seething war against secular schooling in Jerusalem, a tourist from abroad visited R' Yehoshua Leib and witnessed his great zeal. He remained in his home for a long time.

Upon leaving the city, he expressed his amazement and wrote:

> I saw the rav of Brisk for a whole hour. People of embittered hearts and souls, beset by suffering and sickness, came to him, one by one, to receive his blessing, to beg him to pray to revoke the harsh decree from Heaven. The rav commiserated with their pain and suffering. His weak voice softened sweetly and his eyes filled with sympathy. He sat and listened to their sighs and enriched them with his advice and blessing. It was evident that he actually felt their suffering and truly demonstrated what our Sages said that one must feel another's suffering to the extent that he becomes ill from it.
>
> When I rose to go, I happened to innocently touch upon the question of the [secular] schools in Jerusalem. He was transformed in a split second. He arose quivering and became filled with such powerful zeal that all of his bones shook. His mouth breathed fire until he resembled a seraph. His family drew back in fear. The rav had discarded one shape and donned another. Who was man enough to understand the motivation of his conduct and inspiration? It defied my comprehension and that of others.

A SHORT TIME AFTER R' Yehoshua Leib's arrival in Jerusalem, the battle erupted in its full force. The heads of an English movement,

Pines' Challenge

Mazkeret Moshe, became aroused to the need of sending "aid" to the Yishuv in Jerusalem in order to raise its "cultural standard." The organization's aim was to take over the educational institutions of the city by instituting changes and amendments in the spirit of the times.

The heads of the movement were aware of the nature of the Yishuv and of the opposition they could expect. It would not be an easy conquest; Jerusalem Jewry would not allow anyone to touch their most precious asset — the education of the children. They also took into account the fact that the rav from Brisk ruled the city and that he would allow for no compromise in religious matters. They assigned this difficult project to Yechiel Michel Pines, a famous *maskil*, with a considerable following in the Diaspora. His backers hoped that he would prove to be the match for R' Yehoshua Leib.

Pines accepted the challenge and set sail for Palestine.

A small circle of residents labored to make his appearance in their city a festive event. On the eve of his arrival, they generated much activity by cleaning up public areas and decorating synagogues.

Upon his arrival, Pines soon learned that R' Yehoshua Leib could not be circumvented; nothing major or minor could be done behind his back. Pines decided that it would be wiser not to hide what he was doing. He preferred to actually meet with R' Yehoshua Leib and reveal some of his plans. He thought that a direct approach would facilitate his work. It would soften the position of the rabbis towards him and would hush their opposition.

He went to pay his respects to R' Yehoshua Leib and asked to speak privately with him. R' Yehoshua Leib leapt up and hurriedly flung open all the doors and windows of his house, saying, "Let no one say that we shared any secrets together." He continued, "If you have come to ease the burden of the poor of our city, as you promise, fine. But if you have reforms in religion in mind, let me tell you that there is no house and no courtyard from which the sound of Torah does not make itself heard. There is no room for your innovations."

The *maskilim* sought shelter and protection under Pines' wing. They cleaved to him in the hope of finding support for their shaky position. Pines worked hand in hand with these elements. Together, they wrote letters to centers of *Haskalah* in London and other cities, asking for financial aid in what they saw would be a long battle.

Soon after Pines' arrival, someone brought a copy of Pines' *Yaldei Ruchi* to R' Yehoshua Leib. He asked his disciple, R' Yosef Chaim Sonnenfeld, to review it. R' Yosef Chaim agreed with those who viewed the book as being filled with *apikorsus*.

R' Yosef Chaim Sonnenfeld

Some weeks later, Pines was blessed with a son and asked R' Shmuel Salant to be the child's *sandak*. R' Yehoshua Leib learned about this the day before the *bris* and immediately sent a message to R' Shmuel asking him not to participate.

R' Yehoshua Leib's disciple, R' Yosef Chaim Sonnenfeld, acted similarly in a parallel situation. A Jerusalem carpenter, who did occasional work for Pines, was also blessed with a son and asked Pines to be the *sandak*. When R' Yosef Chaim learned of this, he sought out the carpenter's home in one of the dingy alleys of the Old City to try to dissuade him from honoring Pines.

The public was not aware of these undercurrents, as Pines remained engaged in business for the time being. He ordered artistic works in olive wood, which he sent to his friends in London. He pretended to be concerned over the plight of the craftsmen in the city and employed many of them.

But the peace did not last long. Pines had spent his time reconnoitering the spiritual fortress he wished to attack.

Then one fine day, he opened up the doors of a synagogue and *yeshivah* in the Even Yisrael neighborhood. It was open to all who wished to come. If someone asked him what his plans were, he would innocently reply, "I intend to maintain a house of prayer here. I will support ten young men on a monthly stipend to sit and study."

This place soon became a meeting house for *maskilim*, a haven for the teachers and administrators of secular schools and for the "persecuted" in general. The very existence of this "house of study," even though it was beyond the confines of the walls, bode evil for the future.

TAKING UP THE INITIATIVE, R' Yehoshua Leib announced a mass rally to which he summoned the cream of Jerusalem's sages and leaders.

R' Yehoshua Leib Responds

He intended to secure maximum publicity for his cause and wanted to emphatically declare his position regarding the latest developments. On the day of the rally, the public learned that he intended to appear personally, a highly unusual move.

R' Yehoshua Leib was then living in the Kerem section outside the walls. At the appointed hour, he left his home and headed toward the Old City, astride a donkey. The crowds viewed his painful progress as he made his way accompanied by a handful of disciples.

The synagogue hall in the Old City where the meeting had been scheduled was filled to overflowing. There was no discussion or even speeches. The only event was the brief address delivered by R' Yehoshua Leib.

An awed hush fell upon the people assembled in the synagogue, as soon as he appeared. He burned with holy zeal. His very face glowed, as he confronted them and cried out in a tear-choked voice: "Our religion is being threatened by a grave danger. Our Torah is in dire straits. It has come to my attention that Michel Pines has established a special place of worship and prayer. He is an *apikores*, as has been testified before me, and the house which he has designated can only produce *apikorsus*. I therefore forbid visiting it."

This stark plea rent the air.

At the sound of R' Yehoshua Leib's declaration, the audience stood up and enthusiastically drew up a strict ban codifying his words. It was unanimously accepted as binding on all. And with that, the meeting dispersed.

The posters publicizing R' Yehoshua Leib's ban, together with the fact of his appearance in person, struck Pines and his cohorts like a bolt of lightning. Pines called upon several rabbis abroad for support and even published a pamphlet in his own defense, entitled *Shimu Harim Rivi*. But, when it became known that R' Yehoshua Leib was his outspoken opponent, Pines' would-be backers slipped away one by one. Realizing that they were helpless against such an antagonist, even the patrons and colleagues who had sent him ignored Pines' cry for help. They feared further antagonizing the sensibilities of the Jerusalem public.

R' Naftali Tzvi Yehudah Berlin, the Netziv, was approached to defend Pines. His reply was emphatic and unequivocal, "With regard to taking up the defense of Michel Pines, I cannot conceive of anything that could possibly be said contrary to the renowned and revered R' Yehoshua Leib Diskin."

A flood of letters devoted to the ban descended upon R' Yehoshua Leib's house from all over the world. Pines was the brother-in-law of the Karliner Rebbe, R' Pinchas Friedman, whom he begged to come to his aid. In the beginning, the Karliner Rebbe did support him, but it did not take long for him to see Pines' true face. He wrote his brother-in-law:

> I wish to comment on what you wrote in your letter regarding the Sages whose regulations and ordinances, you claim, are their own arbitrary inventions. You say that the laws of *Shemittah* are not viable and can never be fully kept and compare these laws to customs and regulations which exist between bordering countries. The English man of letters, Michel, claims that no countries could possibly enforce such laws; there are always smugglers who deceive the officials. Yet, this is contrary to what our Sages say. In *Semachos*, they sharply criticized those who deceive customs officials and even compare them to *Shabbos* violators, adulterers and idolaters. I am deeply pained to see that the tainted waters which you drank in your youth, and the many secular books you read, have contaminated you to such a degree.

A PROMINENT JERUSALEM PERSONALITY, R' Yitzchak Cheshin, father of R' Yeshaya Cheshin, passed away, leaving a widow and

A Widow's Test

seven orphans. In his lifetime, he had eked out a bare subsistence, and with his passing, the family was totally devastated. The widow lived in the Even Yisrael section, near Michel Pines' home. Seeing her desperate plight, he offered to take the children into his *beis medrash* and to virtually raise them.

The widow went to R' Yehoshua Leib to discuss Pines' offer. R' Moshe Horodner, an elderly, upright Jew, conveyed her question to R' Yehoshua Leib while describing her pitiful circumstances. R' Yehoshua Leib instantaneously rose up in his chair and vehemently explained that he could not permit it. There was an important principle at stake and it could not be sold for money.

The elderly man was about to withdraw, but R' Yehoshua Leib left his seat and accompanied him to the door, saying, "Tell the widow that she has my blessings. She will raise her children to Torah and *chupah* and will enjoy many generations of righteous descendants."

The widow was faithful to R' Yehoshua Leib's decision and held her ground, despite the taunts of a few neighbors who accused her of cruelty to her young children. And she lived to see R' Yehoshua Leib's blessing realized, for she produced generations of outstanding children and established one of the most illustrious families of Jerusalem.

Another incident involved a treasurer of a Jerusalem institution who suddenly fell ill. His acquaintances rushed to R' Yehoshua Leib to ask him to pray for the man.

R' Yehoshua Leib turned to them and said, "He should not have engaged Pines as secretary in that institution." The group repeated their request, stressing that the man was critically ill. But R' Yehoshua Leib reiterated his words and would say no more.

R' Yehoshua Leib took further measures to make sure that Pines was ostracized and that he would have no support from the ranks of Jerusalem rabbis. He once summoned R' Dov Ber Shapira, the loyal attendant of R' Shneur Zalman of Lublin, author of *Toras Chessed*, and commanded him to inform the sage of Lublin that he must not admit Pines into his house. As they were walking, R' Yehoshua Leib suddenly grasped R' Dov Ber's hand and burst out emotionally, "Don't allow that man or his followers to enter your master's house!"

R' Yehoshua Leib's adamant stand brought the battle to its close. Pines' "yeshivah" dwindled and eventually died, due to the ban.

This time the breach had been discovered, and mended, in time. But Pines' "yeshivah" turned out to be only the first of many conflicts. In later years, it was held up as an example of the description of Amalek: "He jumped into a boiling tub. He, himself, was scalded, yet he served to cool it off for the others."

Many who thought that R' Yehoshua Leib was overreacting in claiming that Pines was undermining the very foundations of religious education later admitted that he had indeed been foresighted. A large number went so far as to express regret over not having joined the ranks of the defenders of Torah-true education.

The Ban Renewed

THE STORM SUBSIDED, but other breaches appeared. The *Haskalah* centers abroad continued to pump in funds for the establishment of secular schools in Jerusalem.

Since no parents in the Ashkenazic community were ready to let their children attend such schools, the would-be "enlighteners" concentrated their efforts upon homeless waifs who wandered the streets. Dozens of these street children fell into their clutches.

The founders of those schools were wolves in sheep's clothing. Some even put on both kinds of *tefillin*, were meticulous in their observance of the *mitzvos* and instilled proper Jewish values in their charges. Nevertheless, they slyly insinuated the secular subjects into the school curriculum, cleverly camouflaging their deeds and intentions from the public so that no tangible danger could be seen. Only R' Yehoshua Leib was able to distinguish the full scope of the danger in its inception.

He convened his *beis din* and renewed his earlier ban against such schools. With fiery words he exhorted the public to stand on guard and protect the purity of Torah education. R' Yehoshua Leib's renewal of the ban put a general damper on the *maskilim*'s activities and forced them to go underground and work under the veil of secrecy.

BUT R' YEHOSHUA LEIB DID NOT relax his vigil. He did not consider
the battle completely won nor the enemy altogether routed. He

**The Diskin
Orphanage**
envisioned the need to establish a haven for
abandoned and neglected children. To that end, he
sought to establish a shelter for every orphan and
homeless child, which would provide their needs and would instill in
them the fear of G-d and love for Torah.

To this day, the first association of most people with R' Yehoshua
Leib is the Diskin Orphanage which he founded and which bears his
name. The orphanage was founded to stem the spread of secular
influence in Jerusalem schools and as a counterforce to Dr. Herzberg's
orphanage which stalked orphans and homeless children, gathered
them in and taught them foreign languages. Fearing for the youth
abandoned to such alien supervisors, R' Yehoshua Leib established his
own orphanage to defend against the soul hunters. It served as a house
for every orphaned and homeless child from the Ashkenazic
community.

A declaration was issued in his name that the gates of this house
would be open to every child who lacked a proper education. R'
Yehoshua Leib laid the cornerstone to the edifice in 5640 (1880). In the
summer of 5654 (1894), when it grew too cramped to contain the
growing student body, he purchased a plot of land for the present
orphanage. Such an endeavor was unique in its day, not only in
Jerusalem, but in all of Palestine. Here, orphans and underprivileged
children found housing, clothing and food. Above all, they received a
pure education in the spirit of our Jewish heritage.

R' Yehoshua Leib invested much effort in establishing the
orphanage. He was involved in it from the laying of its foundations to
the placement of the final beam on the roof. Hundreds of children
were rescued from the nets of secular schools thanks to this refuge.
This institution contributed greatly to the religious settlement. It
produced young men who continued to devote their lives to Torah
study and who excelled in *halachah*, as well as laymen loyal to
Hashem and His Torah. Each had the orphanage to thank; if not for it,
they would have been lost.

R' Yehoshua Leib's spirit continued to hover over his orphanage even after his death. The trustees and directors continued to administer it according to his wishes and would not allow any changes to be introduced.

WORD OF THE DISKIN HOME reached the ears of Baron Rothschild in Paris and he sent a considerable sum to R' Yehoshua Leib for its

The Baron's Offer Rejected

upkeep.

When the money reached R' Yehoshua Leib, he asked his disciple, R' Yosef Chaim Sonnenfeld, to send it back to the donor, with a note which read, "Money which comes from a man who also supports secular schools would be better sinking in the ocean than being used. When you cease supporting those other institutions, your donation will be most welcome."

The Baron was incensed by this rejection. R' Mordechai Diskin, a Petach Tikvah farmer and relative of R' Yehoshua Leib, wrote, in his book *Divrei Mordechai*, how, during a three-month stay in Paris, he approached the Baron for financial help in establishing himself as an independent farmer. But Rabbi Lubetzki, a confidant of the Baron, told him that the Baron would not agree to help him, because he was related to R' Yehoshua Leib. Another relative of R' Yehoshua Leib's had already approached him once for assistance, but had been refused.

SEEING THAT R' YEHOSHUA LEIB was determined and that he had full support of the devout, the secularists withdrew for a long time.

The Kollel Regulation

The city was tranquil until 5647 (1887). During the lull, a rumor was circulated to the effect that the ban had been relaxed. The interested parties worked hard to lend credence to the rumor. But R' Yehoshua Leib fought back with a public circular which announced that the ban was still in effect and reiterated the obligation to protest "with all our might against those accursed ones who seek to make a breach."

He called a meeting of the city's leaders at which it was decided that the *kollelim* would withdraw their support from anyone who enrolled a child in the forbidden schools or assisted them in any way. At the end of this meeting, R' Yehoshua Leib rose with fiery zeal, and told all those present, "You must do your utmost for the sake of education!" Trembling, he reiterated his words a second and third time.

The regulation which he then passed concerning the *kollelim* was scrupulously kept throughout his lifetime. After he died, Jerusalemites resolved to uphold it as before, as is evident from one *kollel's* records of 5658 (1898) a few months after R' Yehoshua Leib's death:

> The crown has been removed from our heads. We, the members of Kollel Suwalk and Lomza, lived in his protective shadow and were guided by his holy ways. He steered us and our children away from every impediment and from the pitfalls of the new schools and the rebellious enemies of Hashem. Throughout the time that he was with us, he led us like a faithful shepherd and saved us and our children from the destroyers of the generation and the devouring ones.
>
> Upon his recommendation, the members of the *kollel* abroad gave their support to sustain the worthy poor. Those who veered from the ways of their fathers, the ways of the previous generation, were shunned and denied public office. They lost all claim to the communal treasury down to a penny. Now that the holy ark has been closed, the wicked will rear their heads to wreak havoc upon the safeguards of Israel, to destroy the bastion of faith, to permit the forbidden and nullify the ban of our ancient leaders and let Yaakov be crushed.
>
> Therefore, we, the members of the *kollel*, have rallied as a group to reinforce the original ban of R' Yehoshua Leib Diskin, on us and on all coming generations. Whoever has anything to do with those schools, either by attending them himself or sending his children, or in any other form, shall lose his rights as a member of the Suwalk and Lomza *kollels* and shall be denied as much as a penny from the communal coffer or any public office thereof.
>
> (Signed) The Ninth of *Iyar* 5658, Jerusalem

This document carried the postscript of R' Yosef Chaim Sonnenfeld, who added: "All the signators will be blessed by G-d for having

undertaken to enforce this safeguard of the Torah. The words [of the ban] burn like torches, for this is truly a direct prohibition obligating those who admit the truth and do not deceive themselves."

From the time R' Yehoshua Leib arrived in Jerusalem, not a single person from the Ashkenazic community dared defy the ban. Only some years later did one Yehoshua Y. transgress the ban by enrolling

The Aron Kodesh and bimah in the Churvah Shul

his child into the Kol Yisrael Chaverim school, which, until that time, did not have a single Ashkenazic student.

That Shabbos, two rabbinic delegates appeared in the Churvah synagogue, strode up to the *bimah* and interrupted the prayers to read out the text of the ban which had been issued in 5616 (1866) after Frankel founded the Lemel school. Upon finishing reading the ban, they announced a ban on Yehoshua Y.

Yehoshua Y. owned a store in the Old City. Customers were warned against patronizing that shop and most people complied by staying away. He was also a member of the Suwalk-Lomza *kollel*. His stipend was one hundred sixty-five rubles a year which was now cut off. An additional stipend of twenty napoleons was also denied him upon orders from the Brisker Rav.

Yehoshua Y. was loathe to forgo this income. Taking the initiative, he went abroad and traveled from city to city, — from Lomza to

Suwalk, from Suwalk to Stuchin — to protest the terrible injustice which the *kollel* treasurers in Jerusalem had inflicted upon him. But wherever he went, he was confronted by the same question: "And what does R' Yehoshua Leib have to say about the matter?"

He spent several months in Europe, expending every effort to insure his allocation. He visited numerous local rabbis through whom the *kollel* funds were sent to Jerusalem. He once arrived in Stuchin, a town near Lomza, and laid his plea before R' Yehoshua Heshel Shapira. The rabbi greeted him angrily, saying, "You caused the Brisker Rav to rebuke me. He wrote to me from Jerusalem warning me not to let the abomination — referring to you — enter my home for you were under the ban."

Realizing that his efforts were doomed, Yehoshua Y. finally left the town and returned shamefacedly to Jerusalem, not having accomplished a thing.

R' Moshe Nachum Wallenstein (who later became the *av beis din* of the *Perushim* community in Jerusalem) once gathered a *minyan* for a Friday afternoon *minchah* in the Churvah synagogue courtyard. As he was gathering the *minyan*, Yehoshua Y. happened to pass by. R' Moshe Nachum forgot for a moment who he was and asked him to complete the *minyan*. At the end of the prayers, he approached that tenth man and said, "I asked you to join the *minyan*, but forgot that it is forbidden. So that you do not think that the ban is no longer in effect, I am informing you that in my haste I erred."

WHEN THE SECULARISTS REALIZED that R' Yehoshua Leib was determined and that he intended to block them at every juncture, they adopted a new tactic — force.

The Battle Turns Violent

Once, the founder of the Kol Yisrael Chaverim schools visited *Eretz Yisrael*. Together with his coterie, he came to the Churvah synagogue for *Shabbos* prayers. The students of his school and ragtag street urchins also converged upon the synagogue. They were reinforced by hired hoodlums.

R' Yehoshua Leib ordered three of his disciples, headed by R' Yosef Chaim Sonnenfeld, to restate the ban during the reading of the Torah.

The three did as they were bid. But when they reached the synagogue gates, they were confronted by the gang of hoodlums. R' Yosef Chaim Sonnenfeld was the only one who brushed past them and entered. He pushed his way through the crowd, strode up to the *bimah*, and read the ban aloud. As soon as he was finished, he was attacked by the gangsters who had been waiting for this moment. They pummeled and beat him and pushed him off the stairs of the *bimah* so forcefully that the stairs broke.

The black-and-blue marks from that encounter were visible on his body for a long time afterward. When a colleague remarked upon them a while later, R' Yosef Chaim replied, "These are my battle scars."

Many years later, one of the Kol Yisrael Chaverim school buildings collapsed. Two weeks later, a search among the debris produced a dismembered hand. It was brought to the local rabbi, R' Yosef Tzvi HaLevi, for him to decide what to do. People remembered that one of the elderly teachers of the school had been buried alive under the demolished building.

R' Yosef Tzvi studied the hand and its wristwatch and received witness reports of what that teacher had worn. Then, he suddenly fell down and fainted. When he was revived, he exclaimed, "Look at the far reach of the stern measure of justice! This is the very hand which was raised upon the holy body of R' Yosef Chaim Sonnenfeld when he read out the ban in the Churvah synagogue one *Shabbos* many years ago. Now that hand received its just dessert."

SOME TIME LATER, R' YEHOSHUA LEIB again saw fit to publicize the ban in the city streets. This took place when the Berlin orphanage was

Yet Another Ban

being established in Jerusalem. That institution, headed by Chaim Hirshensohn, was administered as a secular school. This time, R' Leib Chafetz and R' Shlomo Zalman Porush were sent to publicly announce the ban.

When they reached the Lemel school, they were attacked by a gang of hoodlums. R' Shlomo Zalman Porush bore the brunt of their brutality; his skull was fractured and his beard torn out by the roots.

When R' Yehoshua Leib learned of the battle scars R' Shlomo Zalman had earned for his zeal, he paid him a visit and conferred a blessing upon him. From then on, R' Yehoshua Leib exhibited a special affection toward him because of his zealous devotion. When a son was born to R' Shlomo Zalman, R' Yehoshua Leib broke his rule of not accepting honors except in his own home, and attended the *bris*. He was honored as *sandak* and partook of the refreshments, even though he never ate outside his own home.

Upon another occasion, R' Leib Chafetz was again sent by the Brisker Rav to read the ban in the synagogues of Jerusalem. Again, he was attacked by ruffians, who wounded him and had the police arrest him. Still, R' Yehoshua Leib was undaunted. The following day, he sent other messengers to the streets to blow the *shofar* and announce the ban. The messengers continued on to the Western Wall, where they repeated the ban before a large public audience.

The strong-arm tactics did not last long. Those behind this approach saw that they were not achieving their aim; they were not diminishing the opposition to the secular schools. On the contrary, the more brutal their measures, the stronger was the determination to enforce the ban and cast its violators from the community.

R' YEHOSHUA LEIB'S SHARP EYE was fixed upon everything that occurred in the field of education, and was wary and vigilant

A Vigilant Eye

concerning every move in the framework of *chinuch*. He did not overlook matters which the common folk considered inconsequential. The slightest change with even borderline association to education evoked his immediate response.

A wealthy Hungarian Jew once sent a considerable sum to the Kollel Shomrei Hachomos in Jerusalem to be distributed by lots to ten needy scholars.

One of the lucky recipients was a scholar whose grandson was enrolled in a "school." The *kollel* president, R' Yosef Chaim Sonnenfeld, felt that he should be denied the money due to that fact, while R' Shmuel Zanvil Spitzer, a trustee, felt that the grandfather should not be taken to task for the sins of his grandson.

R' Yosef Chaim Sonnenfeld brought the matter before R' Yehoshua Leib, who listened to the arguments, then asked tersely, "Is the grandson in any way supported by his grandfather?" The reply was affirmative. In that case, ruled R' Yehoshua Leib, the latter was not to receive the allocation.

R' Avraham Atkin, an impoverished Jerusalem Torah scholar, was hired for a substantial fee, as the *chazzan* for the High Holiday services in the Lemel school. Afterwards, however, he had second thoughts and went to R' Yehoshua Leib to ask if he had done the right thing.

R' Yehoshua Leib was shocked by the very notion. "You are surely aware that men ostracized by the ban will be praying there, men who are forbidden to be included in a *minyan*." R' Atkin needed to hear no more before revoking the agreement.

Another time, R' Yehoshua Leib was asked to officiate at the wedding of R' Ben Zion Yadler, the famous Jerusalem *maggid*. Under the *chupah*, just as he was about to read the *kesubah*, R' Yehoshua Leib suddenly fled.

The mystery was soon solved. A glance at the document showed that it had been printed by the Lunz press which was affiliated with the *maskilim*. Fearing that the *chassan* was in some way connected with that circle, R' Yehoshua Leib refused to officiate and fled.

The *chassan*'s father ran after R' Yehoshua Leib and explained that his son did not even know the printer. Only when he was absolutely convinced of this did R' Yehoshua Leib agree to return and proceed with the ceremony. However, he insisted that a different *kesubah* be brought; only then did the wedding continue as planned.

R' Yehoshua Leib was strongly opposed to all attempts to promote Hebrew as a spoken language. In 5650 (1890) a language society, *Safah Berurah*, was founded in Jerusalem to promote the use of Hebrew in the land and to support teachers of the Hebrew language.

The heads of the society hired a woman to teach Hebrew to girls. She began with an enrollment of eighteen students. When R' Yehoshua Leib heard of this, he sent her an order to stop the lessons, which she obeyed. Another time, a local scholar, known as "the Hebraist" because he spoke only in Hebrew, came to visit R' Yehoshua

Leib. "The Hebraist" was a *talmid chacham*, who studied all day wearing his *tallis* and *tefillin*. As was his habit, he addressed R' Yehoshua Leib in Hebrew. As soon as the first words left his mouth, R' Yehoshua Leib made it clear that he would not continue the conversation and asked the man to leave.

R' Yehoshua Leib was also vehemently opposed to journals published by *maskilim*. He never read a newspaper in his life and would not allow one into his house. R' S. Shenker once came to show R' Yehoshua Leib a certain article in *Hatzefirah*, which he wanted to comment upon in writing. Noticing the newspaper in his hand, R' Yehoshua Leib became incensed and told him, "Remove that newspaper from my house! It is tainted!"

A certain Berlin rabbi wrote an attack against Jerusalem's "zealots" for persecuting Chaim Hirshensohn, a principal of a secular school in the Holy City. His article was published in the Jewish newspapers. The article both defended Hirshensohn and attacked his "fanatic" opponents. Since the rabbi was a well-respected figure, the article created quite a stir.

One local zealot could not contain himself and came out with a caustic and disrespectful broadside against the rabbi from Berlin. Contained in this counterattack was the name of a Jerusalem rabbi, who was cited as if he supported the views of the author. In due course, the letter was circulated in the Diaspora and reached its intended address — the author of the original article. He wrote to the Jerusalem rabbi mentioned in the counterattack and the latter felt obliged to make a public apology.

When R' Yehoshua Leib learned that the Jerusalem rabbi wished to publicly deny having had anything to do with the sharp letter, he asked him not to do so. Hearing that R' Yehoshua Leib was assuming responsibility for the letter or at least offering the writer his protection, he desisted and kept silent.

A group of disgruntled men, women and children of the secular camp once congregated in his courtyard to protest R' Yehoshua Leib's opposition to a Jerusalem hospital which was administered by *maskilim*. They raised a furor, claiming that his opposition would cause the hospital — one of the few serving the Jerusalem public — to shut down. R' Yehoshua Leib stepped out on his balcony and silenced the mob, explaining that a war for the soul of Jerusalem was going on and that the community had to remain strong in defense of its spiritual life.

NEARING HIS EIGHTIETH YEAR, R' Yehoshua Leib found it necessary to sign the ban on secular studies yet a third time. On *erev Shabbos*, 7

The Final Ban

Adar, 5656 (1896), he wrote: "The ban has not been modified by as much as a hairsbreadth, nor is any person empowered to abolish it, for it was established by *tzaddikim* of an earlier generation, pillars of Judaism. Were all the sages of Jewry to unite, they would be powerless to budge it an inch."

R' Shmuel Salant, rav of Jerusalem, and R' Shneur Zalman, *av beis din* of Lublin, also affixed their signatures to this declaration and appended their own reiterations of the ban. The proclamation of Jerusalem's three elders was circulated throughout the Diaspora.

The newspapers of the *maskilim* abroad raised a furor against the drastic measures which R' Yehoshua Leib was employing in his battle against secular schools. Zionistic and nationalist writers heaped scorn upon the Old Yishuv in their usual acerbic style.

R' Yehoshua Leib was successful in his long campaign and saw the fruits of his efforts over his twenty-one years in Jerusalem. His last day was approaching and his pure eyes saw Jerusalem burgeoning with the hand of Orthodox Jewry uppermost. Its *chadarim* were intact; the population upheld the ban against secular schools faithfully.

R' Yehoshua Leib, however, did not see himself free of his responsibility. He continued to be on the alert to his very last moments. From his confined room, he feared that in his absence the barriers might slowly crumble. He attempted to set the demarcation lines for all time.

And if today, many marvel at the secret strength of the Old Yishuv community which has continued to preserve its independent educational system, and ask themselves who fanned that great fire so deep in the hearts of the people that it continues to burn, the only answer is: R' Yehoshua Leib.

NOR WAS EDUCATION the only area in which R' Yehoshua Leib played a leading role in defending against any changes in traditional religious practice.

Shemittah

Until 5649 (1889), *Shemittah* had never been an issue for the religious Yishuv or *Eretz Yisrael*. It did not occur to anyone to seek a way out. The commandment was a fact of life.

But in 5648 (1888), the eve of the sabbatical year, the topic of *Shemittah* suddenly became "the *problem* of *Shemittah*."

The supervisors of Baron Rothschild, who owned vast tracts of land in *Eretz Yisrael*, feared for the consequences of not harvesting the land, which supported so many families. This consideration had not existed in previous *Shemittah* years. The agents of the Baron turned to rabbis abroad for a solution to the problem.

A violent halachic struggle erupted. One side categorically forbade working the land in any form. The other camp found a provisional opening for that year only. The controversy involved most of the great scholarly minds abroad and the deliberations grew more heated as *Shemittah* approached.

The first *heter* bore the signatures of R' Yisrael Yehoshua Kutna and R' Shmuel ben HaRav R' Yehoshua Leib Bialystock Shmuel Zanvil, *moreh tzedek* of Warsaw. Upon the release of this *heter*, R' Yitzchak Elchanan Spector, *av beis din* of Kovno, and the leading European *posek* of the period, issued his own *heter*.

As soon as R' Yitzchak Elchanan's *heter* was publicized, the rabbis of Jerusalem called a meeting and issued a prohibition against any form of farming or related works during *Shemittah*, without exception.

R' Yehoshua Leib, together with R' Shmuel Salant, rav of Jerusalem, issued a declaration that "there is no sanction to plow, sow, harvest or plant, either oneself or by means of a non-Jew, aside from those activities which help preserve trees."

Word of R' Yehoshua Leib's ruling reached the Diaspora and put a swift end to the discussion and the controversy. R' Yosef Dov Ber Soloveitchik of Brisk, R' David Friedman of Karlin, the Netziv of Volozhin, R' Yosef Zecharya Stern, and the Ridvaz all came out in support of his ruling.

At this time, R' Elya Chaim Meisel of Lodz and a rabbi who favored a lenient ruling happened to visit the home of a wealthy Jew in Warsaw. In the presence of many distinguished men, the rav of Lodz declared that one could not overrule a local rabbi's decision in his sphere of jurisdiction. Since R' Yehoshua Leib Diskin had already made his opinion public, he did not see how it could be opposed. The rabbi accompanying R' Elya Chaim disagreed.

R' Meisel responded sharply, "We are forbidden to determine the law for the farmers in the face of the Brisker Rav's ruling, for he is the leader of the entire Diaspora. All of us rabbis are like a garlic peel in comparison. Who are we to oppose him?"

The Ridvaz, *av beis din* of Slutzk, bitterly condemned those few farmers who refused to adhere to the prohibition. He wrote: "Let it be known that violating the first *Shemittah* in 5648 caused Hashem to send a plague of locust the following year so that all the grain was wiped out."

R' Yehoshua Leib wrote to Baron Rothschild begging him not to seek loopholes and leniencies:

> Several months ago some devout Jews came to me to seek permission to engage in agricultural labors during the Sabbatical Year. I swore to them that I would never lend my hand to such a thing.
>
> Surely they could have realized that it would not augment your good name to seek *heterim* throughout the four corners of the earth. The Almighty has bestowed upon Your Excellency a heritage in the Holy Land and has enabled you to rebuild the ruins of close to two thousand years. It follows that observing the Sabbatical Year would enhance your honor, both among the Jews and the nations of the world. All would congratulate you for establishing your colonies upon the laws of the Torah, as they were given at Sinai. Were that the case, a cry of jubilation would rise up in the Holy Land, the sound of joy from the Holy City.
>
> I am certain that the blessing written in the Torah which awaits the one who properly observes *Shemittah*, "And I shall command My blessing," will be fulfilled with respect to you in

Paris, too, and in all of your endeavors will G-d raise you and make you great. And may Your Excellency's eyes, and ours, see the coming of the Redeemer, speedily and in our days.

The majority of farmers in the Holy Land heeded R' Yehoshua Leib's opinion and withstood the difficult trial.

In the next *Shemittah*, in 5656 (1896), the rabbi of Jaffa, R' Naftali Hertz, devised a new *heter* based on selling trees to a non-Jew to free their fruits from the prohibition of marketing and commerce. But even he did not do so wholeheartedly, for he later wrote: "I saw that those who were seeking a way out of the laws of *Shemittah* did not gain thereby in the long run. I also was punished for tampering with *Shemittah* and I am now ill due to it. I greatly fear to make permanent inroads and to rule leniently in such a weighty matter."

CHAPTER SEVEN

His Character Traits

HROUGHOUT HIS LIFE, R' Yehoshua Leib Diskin tried to conceal his spiritual greatness. But he could not succeed totally in this task anymore than he could hide his greatness in Torah.

His Modesty

From the very first day he set foot in Jerusalem, R' Yehoshua Leib's complete lack of any need to demonstrate his greatness in Torah was a source of wonder. He arrived in Av 5637 (1877). All of Jerusalem, led by R' Meir Auerbach, the Kalisher *av beis din*, and R' Shmuel Salant, rav of the city, went out to greet the Brisker Rav and accord him a royal welcome. R' Auerbach addressed the crowd with a complicated and cleverly structured speech. R' Yehoshua Leib listened in silence. The Kalisher Rav carried on with his *pilpul*, building and demolishing, proposing and rejecting. Still, R' Yehoshua Leib kept silent. The audience was almost led to think that this complex structure was beyond his grasp.

A few days later, this same scene repeated itself. A delegation of scholars from the Sephardic community went to R' Yehoshua Leib's house to pay their respects. One of the rabbis launched into an elaborate and lengthy *pilpul*. R' Yehoshua Leib gave no indication that he understood what they were talking about; he made no comment whatsoever. The Sephardic rabbis, who had heard so much about his greatness and scholarship, left his home sorely disappointed.

When R' Yehoshua of Kutna came to live in Jerusalem, he went to pay his respects to R' Yehoshua Leib. He, too, began the conversation with a scholarly dissertation, but to his great surprise, R' Yehoshua Leib showed no interest. He merely sat and listened in silence.

On another occasion, R' Shneur Zalman of Lublin, author of *Toras Chessed*, married a second time. The cream of Jerusalem's scholars flocked to the wedding. R' Yehoshua Leib was asked to officiate, with R' Shmuel Salant and R' Yaakov Shaul Elyashar, the *Rishon LeZion*, reciting the blessings.

After the ceremony, the guests gathered around the food-laden tables. The rav of Lublin presented an involved *pilpul* with the guests adding their comments here and there. Only R' Yehoshua Leib sat in utter silence, without reacting.

After he returned home, he was visited by R' Tzvi Michel Shapira who suggested that R' Yehoshua Leib's silence might have disturbed the rav of Lublin. And he added, people might think that R' Yehoshua Leib had not understood the subject matter.

R' Yehoshua Leib nodded and said, "As a matter of fact, I enjoyed his *pilpul*, but felt that I had nothing to add or detract from it." He proceeded to repeat the *pilpul* verbatim.

R' Yaakov Orenstein, one of R' Yehoshua Leib's favorite disciples, aptly defined his master's humility: "When great men used to come to

R' Yaakov Shaul Elyashar

him, he would hide his scholarship and sit in silence. And when young men came to ask him questions in *halachah* or sought the explanation of difficult topics, he would teach them from the text, explaining with great clarity, making sure that the questioner fully understood his answer."

His Patience

R' YEHOSHUA LEIB ONCE PRESENTED his disciples with a complex mathematical calculation. Later, an unlearned man begged him to explain what he had just taught. Patiently, he sat him down in front of all his *talmidim* and explained it thoroughly from beginning to end.

On *motzaei Shabbos*, R' Yehoshua Leib would expound upon the weekly portion. His audience usually included two or three simple folk. Whenever they posed what they considered to be a difficult question, he would treat it with all seriousness and answer it to their satisfaction.

A Rumanian shoemaker often came to him with such "scholarly problems." Sometimes, his comments aroused mockery and disdain. But R' Yehoshua Leib always treated them with due respect, ever careful not to embarrass the questioner. He would repeat the question for the benefit of his listeners, consider it from different angles and then finally come up with a suitable answer, as if after considerable mental exertion.

Once he extended his lesson longer than usual. An elderly man became tired and rose to go home. R' Yehoshua Leib, too, got up, caught up with him and gave him his arm. He led him down the stairs until the gate, explaining that one should not let such an old man go down alone late at night.

Heaven Must Have Punished Me

R' MOSHE SHOCHET, WHO HAD BEEN a *sofer* in his youth, once came to R' Yehoshua Leib with a *mezuzah* which appeared to have an error in Hashem's Name. At first, R' Yehoshua Leib refused to rule upon it and referred him to other authorities in the city. But upon R' Moshe's insistence, he finally offered him three solutions how to deal with the *mezuzah*. Suddenly, he realized that the third way was not correct. He leaped up, grasped his head in both hands and rushed frantically to a corner of the room, tears streaming from his eyes. He attributed this error to his having at first put the man off. Trying to make amends, he went over to R' Shochet, put a hand on his shoulder and said, "Heaven must have punished me for not replying to your question at once."

UPON R' YEHOSHUA LEIB DISKIN'S ARRIVAL in Jerusalem, several young men, astute and prestigious scholars, approached him, implor-

Forty Days on a Daf

ing him to give a regular lecture. R' Yehoshua Leib agreed and began a daily *shiur* in *Bava Basra*. Throughout the summer of 5638 (1878), they covered no more than three pages of *Gemara*.

A single phrase in a *Tosafos* once occupied them for three consecutive days, and a single *daf* (page), forty days. Seeing that his students felt confident that they knew the *daf* thoroughly, R' Yehoshua Leib said to them, "It is a mistake to think that we fully comprehend this page of *Gemara*. We are like young children groping about with our limited intellects. But what can we do? To dwell any longer on this page is impossible, for what will happen to the rest of the Torah? We should bear in mind, however, that we are still far from even understanding the simple meaning. Who are we? What are we?" he concluded with a mournful sigh. "As David said, 'Open my eyes that I may see.' "

Then R' Yehoshua Leib proceeded to expound upon that one page of *Gemara* with such simplicity and clarity that the smallest iota of complacency or vainglory that might still have existed in anyone's heart melted into nothingness. One of those who attended the class, R' Yaakov Orenstein, described it as follows: "One might think that he taught his students the acrobatics of *pilpul* and razor-sharp logic. Rather, he concentrated upon the words of *Rashi* and *Tosafos* and taught us how to analyze the wording. Whoever heard him, saw and understood that he was plunging into the depths of the vast Talmudic sea, the captain surrounded by mighty waves."

The series of *shiurim* lasted throughout the summer months, four hours straight, every day including Friday and *Shabbos* (except for *erev Yom Kippur*, which was made up for that evening after the evening prayers).

During that entire span, R' Yehoshua Leib never asked a question, brought an answer or interjected any explanation from a different source. He did not utilize any reference sources outside of the very topic under study.

Each year, on the night of his father's *yahrzeit*, R' Yehoshua Leib would assemble his disciples after the evening prayers and study *mishnayos* with them. They would not cover even one *mishnah*, though they studied through the night until dawn!

Sometimes, he would devote weeks to one paragraph in the *Shulchan Aruch*.

SOMEONE ONCE VISITED R' Yehoshua Leib and noted the dozens of birds flitting about his home. The man reminded him of the *Gemara*

Who Says They're Kosher?

in *Sanhedrin* (111): "Kosher birds make their nests by *tzaddikim*." R' Yehoshua Leib modestly replied, "What makes you so sure that these are kosher birds?"

R' YEHOSHUA LEIB PREFERRED to remain out of the limelight. He lived abstemiously, in a simple two-room dwelling, with the simplest

A Servant Needs No More

of furniture. He refused to benefit from others and never accepted a gift. He invested considerable effort in hiding his true spiritual stature from his contemporaries. Not only did he reject the offer to serve as rav of Jerusalem made upon his arrival, he also rejected the offer of comfortable lodgings.

A group of tourists once came to visit him on *Yom Tov* and asked him why he chose to live in such squalor. He rose, flung open a window and pointed to the desolate Temple Mount, saying, "A servant need not ask for more than his Master."

But they continued to press him, "Does it do credit to your Torah knowledge to live in such wretched surroundings?" He replied, "You are mistaken in considering me a great scholar. The little I have achieved is only due to my determination to live in poverty and self-restraint."

ONCE, R' YEHOSHUA LEIB CHANGED his dwelling place. On moving day, he accompanied the porter, who was carrying his writings,

The Father Takes Precedence
contained in two boxes. To the amazement of passersby, R' Yehoshua Leib followed the porter all the way. At each step, he repeatedly reminded him to be careful not to change the order of the boxes.

The porter could not understand his great anxiety and asked, "And what would be so terrible if I did change the order of the boxes?" R' Yehoshua Leib explained, "The upper box contains my father's novellae, the lower one mine. It is not fitting for my writings to be on top of my father's!"

HIS DISCIPLE, R' ZORACH BRAVERMAN, once happened to be in R' Yehoshua Leib's home late at night when suddenly he heard a train.

Unprepared for *Mashiach*
The Jerusalem railroad had just recently been opened and R' Yehoshua Leib was not familiar with the sound of its tooting. He suddenly grew fearful. Sighing deeply, he said, "They are already clearing the way. So soon. The time of Redemption is approaching. [He probably based his assumption on the saying that before *Mashiach* arrives, the ways will be cleared.] But we are not yet ready."

R' Yehoshua Leib repeated himself three times, his entire body shaking in awe. He, the leader of the generation, considered himself unprepared.

THOUGH HE WAS EXTREMELY self-effacing with regard to his own person, he reacted vehemently to the slightest affront to another

The Honor of a *Talmid Chacham*
talmid chacham. He made a special point of honoring those who devoted their whole life to study.

While R' Yehoshua Leib was rav in Lomza, his younger brother, R' Avraham Shmuel Diskin, rav of Plonsk, invalidated a *kesubah* (marriage contract) on the grounds that the witnesses' signatures were too far from the body of the document.

Just to be certain, R' Avraham Shmuel referred the question to R' Yosef Shaul Natansohn, the *av beis din* of Lvov, who upheld the original ruling.

R' Yehoshua Leib heard about the matter. He feared that R' Avraham Tchechenover, the esteemed rav of Tchechenov, where the marriage had taken place, might take offense over the whole incident. R' Yehoshua Leib traveled to Tchechenov to speak to him personally. As it happened, R' Avraham had had nothing to do with the *kesubah* in question, but R' Yehoshua Leib's concern with his honor made an impact on the whole district.

While serving in Lomza, the *chazzan* of nearby Stuchin raised his hand against the *av beis din*. R' Yehoshua Leib demanded that the man be removed at once.

His distress over the disgrace of a Torah scholar can be discerned from a letter which he wrote at that time to a friend, R' Yehoshua Heschel Ashkenazi, rav of Lublin:

> To my dear friend, the famous, renowned rabbi, scion of a great family, Moreinu HaRav Yehoshua Heschel Ashkenazi, *av beis din* of Lublin:
>
> I shall not deny that I was horrified to hear of the travesty which took place in Stuchin when a newcomer forcefully edged out the *chazzan*, an upright man, from his post and instituted himself into that office. When the *av beis din* objected, that wicked man dared raise a fist against him, causing blood to flow, Heaven forfend! The *av beis din* forbade him from leading the prayers, but he ignored him and did so, anyway. Then our good friend, the *av beis din* of Warsaw, zealously defended the honor of the Torah. I concurred and was joined by all the rabbis of the region. We forbade the man from serving as *chazzan* ever again until he comes contritely to ask forgiveness. We did not hesitate to judge him in his absence since the *av beis din* had already ruled likewise. As for the technical details about judging someone *in absentia*, I have studied the matter and can provide the reasoning behind it on request.

He now boasts that he acquired a *heter* from you, but I refused to believe him. Perhaps you wrote it by way of argumentation and not as a halachic ruling or were not informed of all the details of the incident. If you did give them a real *heter*, I ask you to retract it for the sake of that Torah scholar's honor. They must have fed you misinformation, for the [*av beis din* of Stuchin] served as *dayan* for close to forty years. I request that you clarify your position on the matter.

I consider that upstart *chazzan* as not far removed from an *apikores* for having distressed a scholar and for having lowered the honor of Torah to the dust and paved the way for others to defy and denigrate. May *Hashem* break their pride and restore the peace.

WHEN ASKED BY SOMEONE from a different city to rule upon a certain question, he refused, out of respect for the local rav. He wrote,

Do Not Set Yourself up as a Man

"I received your two letters but will not reply to your question in keeping with the saying of our Sages in *Berachos*, 'In a place that has a man [of authority], do not set yourself up as a man.' Your rav is fully qualified to reply to your question."

When asked for his opinion upon a matter that others had already ruled upon, he declined to reply. He feared that by intervening, he might insult or embarrass the scholars who had already been involved.

During his residence in Jerusalem, R' Yehoshua Leib usually referred questions brought to him to R' Shmuel Salant, the rav of the city. Even when a question arose in his own home, he would send for R' Shmuel's opinion.

Once, when he took a short stroll outside the city to refresh himself, one of his escorts made a remark which could be interpreted as slighting R' Shmuel Salant. R' Yehoshua Leib turned pale and receded four cubits backward. When the speaker saw his strong reaction, he fell to the ground and accepted his master's formal rebuke, according to the laws of one who shames a *talmid chacham*.

When people referred to R' Meir Leibush Malbim simply as "the

Malbim," R' Yehoshua Leib would protest and demand the addition of "Rav."

IN LOMZA, HE MADE SURE that the *yeshivah* students were assigned to eat their meals at the homes of people who respected and

The Honor of a *Yeshivah* *Bachur*

appreciated Torah scholars. Upon learning that one host was not treating his student-guest with the proper deference, he summoned the man to his home and scolded him accordingly.

One of the communal leaders of Jerusalem was once sitting at R' Yehoshua Leib's table, when a poor, shabbily dressed young *kollel* student entered the room. R' Yehoshua Leib stood up while the *askan* remained seated. R' Yehoshua Leib objected and told him, "Stand up for this *ben yeshivah!*"

At one point, R' Yehoshua Leib decided to remove all the benches from his private study. All that remained was a single chair at the head of the table. As soon as a Torah scholar would enter, R' Yehoshua Leib would ask that a chair be brought for him. This was his way of showing respect to his visitor.

A rich man from Bialystock once came to R' Yehoshua Leib when he was rav of Lomza and asked him to select an outstanding young man for his daughter. R' Yehoshua Leib pointed out a promising youth of fifteen. The rich man engaged him in scholarly conversation but was sorely disappointed when the youth was unable to explain one of the Maharsha's comments in *Kesubos*.

When R' Yehoshua Leib learned the reason for his disappointment, he sent for the rich man and began conversing with him. He purposely confused him so that when he asked him to explain the Maharsha, he was unable to do so. "See!" said R' Yehoshua Leib. "Neither you understand it, nor do I. And yet you wanted the boy of fifteen to comprehend that difficult Maharsha? Nevertheless, I tell you that he is destined to become a *gadol*, a truly great scholar!"

The rich man conceded and agreed to take the boy as a son-in-law on the condition that R' Yehoshua Leib review an entire tractate of the Maharsha's commentary with him. The boy eventually became such a prominent scholar that his father-in-law was unable to understand his everyday conversation.

EVERY PAIN THAT AFFLICTED a Torah scholar affected him directly. In *Iyar* 5638 (1878), R' Meir Auerbach, former rav of Kalish, became

A Clock Replaced

mortally ill. He lay writhing in pain. R' Yehoshua Leib, accompanied by R' Moshe Shochet, went to visit him. After his visit, the rav of Kalish testified that he had not removed his gaze from R' Yehoshua Leib's face the entire time and knew that he was suffering deeply along with him.

The elderly *Maggid* of Vilkomir settled in Jerusalem toward the end of his days. Early one morning, when he was away in the synagogue, burglars entered his home and stole his clock.

On her way to work, R' Yehoshua Leib's washerwoman heard about the theft and happened to mention it to the *rebbetzin* within her husband's earshot. He called to his wife and said, "Sarah, find out what kind of clock was stolen and go buy an exact replica so that we can replace it before the *Maggid* learns of the loss."

R' Yehoshua Leib later explained that any anxiety or grief for a man of the *Maggid's* age — he was then more than one hundred years old — might shorten his life and must be prevented at all costs.

HE COMPLETELY FULFILLED the commandment of loving his fellow Jew. His disciple, R' Yaakov Orenstein, described R' Yehoshua Leib's

Feeling Another's Pain

ahavas Yisrael: "We saw with our own eyes how he literally participated in the pain of every individual Jew. He truly fulfilled the positive commandment of loving one's neighbor as oneself."

An impoverished woman once came to R' Yehoshua Leib to ask him to pray for her young son, who was in critical condition. He agreed, and asked her to bring him news on his progress. When the boy began improving, the woman returned to him. Before she had even reached his door, the neighbors in that courtyard rushed up to her to ask how her son was feeling. She replied joyfully that he was much better. Just then R' Yehoshua Leib appeared in the doorway. Hearing the good news, he raised his hands toward Heaven and cried out, "Blessed is He and blessed is His Name!"

A perennially despondent beggar once came to him to ask him to pray for his daughter who had become deaf. R' Yehoshua Leib lifted his eyes heavenward and sighed deeply, praying, "Don't inflict a double burden."

IN 5639 (1879), JERUSALEM WAS HIT by famine. Families were starving. In many homes, there was not even a crust of bread. The hunger was so intense that one day two men collapsed in the Churvah synagogue and died before they could be brought to the hospital.

The Soup Kitchen

R' Yehoshua Leib was galvanized into organizing rescue work. He had a soup kitchen set up which was open to everyone. He created shelters for the poor by renting and furnishing several apartments and founded a benevolent society called *Moshav Zekeinim veChonenei Dalim* for the poor and elderly, the homeless and hungry.

Another time, the Warsaw *kollel* in Jerusalem became embroiled in internal conflict as a result of slander. In the ensuing financial crisis, dozens of families in the Old Yishuv reached the brink of starvation, since they subsisted on the *kollel* allocations and these had now stopped.

R' Yehoshua of Kutna and his son-in-law, R' Chaim Elazar Wax, rav of Pietrokov, had just come to Jerusalem at the time. They decided to investigate the matter thoroughly. R' Yehoshua Leib turned to the rav of Kutna and said, "I wish to confer upon you the blessing which Moshe gave to Yehoshua: 'May Hashem save you from the counsel of the spies who speak ill of the Land.' "

The rav of Kutna understood the implications of this blessing. He strengthened himself against the slanderers and did not leave Jerusalem until he had straightened the matter out and restored the stipend to the *kollel* families.

R' Yehoshua Leib once learned that his beloved disciple, R' Yosef Chaim Sonnenfeld, was in very difficult circumstances. Aware that R' Yosef Chaim would not knowingly accept any charity, he had a sum of money inserted in a crack of the door. R' Chaim guessed that his teacher must be behind the surreptitious gift and accepted his help.

R' Yehoshua Leib's self-sacrifice in helping others was especially highlighted with respect to his orphanage; he loved its charges boundlessly. When taking his evening walk, he would bend down to gather twigs and branches along the way. He stuffed them into his pockets exclaiming, "This wood will make good fuel to heat the orphanage and feed the unfortunate children there." When the *rebbetzin* learned of this, she sewed a special pocket into his coat which he continued to fill upon his nightly walks.

The Milkman's Secret

LOCATED AMONG THE ARAB FRUIT VENDORS on Shalshelet Street in the Old City was one Reb Yechezkel Lilienthal, a devout, upright Jew who was accorded the privilege of supplying R' Yehoshua Leib with vegetables. Reb Yechezkel contracted tuberculosis, and the illness sapped his strength little by little. His business dwindled to nothing. To the family's surprise, the Jerusalem milkman, Reb David Goldberg, offered to bring the greengrocer a quantity of fresh goats' milk, which was known to be especially beneficial for tuberculosis sufferers, each day. The milkman continued to supply the milk for a long time without accepting money.

On the day that R' Yehoshua Leib passed away, the supply stopped. Only then did the family learn that he had been paying for the milk from his own pocket without anyone's knowledge.

When R' Yehoshua Leib was approached to pray on behalf of an ill person, he did so without delay. Once, right before *Rosh Hashanah*, a man rushed into his home begging that R' Yehoshua Leib pray that he have children. In the middle of the holiday, R' Yaakov Orenstein went to the man's house to inform him that he had heard R' Yehoshua Leib mention him in his prayers.

Salt in His Tea

HE WAS ESPECIALLY CAREFUL not to cause people even a hint of embarrassment or pain. Every *motzaei Shabbos*, R' Yehoshua Leib would expound upon the weekly portion before a group of people in his home. His attendant would prepare tea for all those who attended. Once, the attendant mistook the salt container for the sugar bowl and inadvertently put salt into his tea. Since R' Yehoshua Leib's doctor had prescribed that he use large amounts of sugar to increase his energy, the *shammash* put several heaping spoons of the salt into the glass. He sipped the contents of the glass without showing the slightest sign of distaste.

It was the *rebbetzin* who discovered the error. She ran into the room shouting, "There's salt in your tea!" The glass was cleared away and returned to the kitchen. When his students tasted the dregs of that glass, they marveled at his self-restraint in having drank the unquaffable tea to avoid embarrassing the poor *shammash*.

After everyone left, the *rebbetzin* asked her husband how he had allowed himself to drink the contents of the glass knowing that it might be harmful to his health.

"What?" he wondered, "And shame a Jew in public?"

Reb Leib, an elderly Jerusalemite, ate his meals at R' Yehoshua Leib's table for a period of time, but found it difficult to eat bread, since most of his teeth were missing. When R' Yehoshua Leib saw his suffering, he sat Reb Leib next to him and would slice the bread, separate the soft part from the crust and give it to him, slice after slice, with fatherly concern.

Another time, R' Yehoshua Leib invited a convert to eat at his table. He exhibited a remarkable affection towards the man, thus fulfilling the commandment to love the convert with all his heart and soul.

One of R' Yehoshua Leib's disciples was charged with guarding the wheat which he used for *matzos*. One year, the disciple passed away, and R' Yehoshua Leib's relatives suggested that he remove the wheat from his house and transfer it to another disciple's safekeeping. R' Yehoshua Leib, however, would not hear of it: such an act, he explained, would add to the bereaved widow's already painful loss.

The physical pain of any Torah scholar was felt deeply by R' Yehoshua Leib. When he learned that R' Yosef Chaim Sonnenfeld fasted throughout the Ten Days of Penitence, he let him know that he objected. He even visited him at home during this time and ordered him to eat and drink.

Another time, R' Yehoshua Leib learned that R' Zevulun Charlap, who was then the administrator of the Suwalk *kollel*, was living in dire poverty and refused to take wages for his work. He summoned him and commanded him to take a monthly salary. Otherwise, he warned, he, too, would forfeit his monthly *kollel* stipend. Upon hearing this, R' Zevulun agreed to accept a salary.

JUST AS R' YEHOSHUA LEIB could not bear to see a Torah scholar suffer bodily pain, so was he distressed at another's spiritual suffering.

Not Forcing His Will

He never conferred a position of honor on a scholar if he knew that it was genuinely against his wishes.

When R' Yehoshua Leib founded his *beis din* in Jerusalem, he appointed R' Yosef Chaim Sonnenfeld as its head. But the appointment deeply distressed R' Yosef Chaim, who fled from honor or anything resembling it. R' Yosef Chaim made only one request of his master: R' Yehoshua Leib was to relieve him of his duties as soon as a suitable replacement could be found.

Seeing that R' Yosef Chaim was sincere in his request, R' Yehoshua Leib complied. About a month later, R' Yaakov Leib Levi succeeded him as *av beis din* and R' Yosef Chaim Sonnenfeld was released from the yoke which so oppressed him.

When R' Koppel Shapira, treasurer of the Suwalk *kollel*, passed away, R' Yehoshua Leib wanted to appoint his son, R' Tzvi Michel, as his successor. R' Tzvi Michel, however, became distraught upon hearing the news. He could not conceive of disobeying his master. Yet the very thought of accepting a time-consuming public office was abhorrent to him. He could not spare precious time from Torah study.

R' Tzvi Michel gathered a group of ten outstanding scholars and had them study all night for his sake. Just before dawn, he took them to the Western Wall to pray that the Almighty change his master's decision.

The group's prayers were answered, for when the Brisker Rav heard about it and realized how much R' Tzvi Michel was opposed to the idea, he summoned him and said, "I thought the matter over and decided that it was asking too much. I am releasing you from that responsibility."

R' Yehoshua Leib was extremely cautious not to cause a Torah scholar the slightest distress or to make him alter any religious practice which he had accepted upon himself. R' David Shutak, a famous

The Western Wall, c. 1900

Jerusalemite, refrained from speaking. He once needed R' Yehoshua Leib's advice on some matter and thought it disrespectful not to speak. But to his surprise, R' Yehoshua Leib greeted him and immediately told him to write out his request on paper, thus sparing him mental anguish.

R' YEHOSHUA LEIB WAS WARY of all ruses to place gifts into his household. Many people tried to find ways to slip money through

He Who Scorns Gifts Will Live

open windows or side doors, but he was ever wise to their ways and succeeded in never benefiting from such attempts.

He also refused to accept any free service. If he needed someone's help, but the benefactor refused to be paid for his assistance, R' Yehoshua Leib would not agree to accept his services.

His young son, R' Yitzchak Yerucham, once became ill and was forbidden to exert himself mentally. R' Yehoshua Leib asked one of his students to keep the boy company during his illness, stressing the fact that he intended to pay him for his "work." What was the reward he chose? He agreed to study privately with him during the evenings of those days he spent at his son's bedside.

As a young man, R' Moshe Grosbard often ate at R' Yehoshua Leib's table. He once found R' Yehoshua Leib standing alone in the kitchen, boiling water. R' Moshe took the kettle from him, set it on the flame, and made him a glass of tea. R' Yehoshua Leib would not accept this service "free." He rose to his feet and blessed him with long life.

The *rebbetzin* once hired a Jewish porter to deliver a package to her home. When it arrived, she paid the man and he went on his way. Later that day, R' Yehoshua Leib noticed the large package standing in the hallway and asked about it. His wife explained that she had hired a porter to bring it to the house. R' Yehoshua Leib was silent for a moment, making mental calculations. He concluded that according to the bulk of the load, the porter should have received a higher fee. He took out some coins and sent out a messenger to pay the porter his rightful earnings.

It was late at night. The messenger walked through the dark alleys in search of the man. He finally found him and gave him the extra money which R' Yehoshua Leib had sent.

R' Moshe Jules, a devout Jerusalemite scholar and druggist, treated R' Yehoshua Leib whenever he was ill, earning his devotion and admiration.

R' Yehoshua Leib begged him to accept a few coins for his services but R' Moshe persistently refused, since he dispensed his drugs free to all. When R' Yehoshua Leib saw how determined he was not to accept anything, he called him over and said, "R' Moshe, I can't have you caring for me without payment. At least give me the privilege of serving you a glass of tea each time you come to my home." From that time on, R' Yehoshua Leib made sure to bring R' Moshe a glass of tea every time he visited and R' Moshe accepted this "payment." As he advanced in age and became weaker, he required more frequent treatment. He found it necessary to raise R' Moshe's "fee." This time he offered to teach R' Moshe anything that he wished to know on any Torah-related subject. R' Moshe happily accepted these new terms and continued to care for R' Yehoshua Leib devotedly up until his last day.

R' MOSHE JULES ONCE CAME to visit R' Yehoshua Leib and found him lying in bed, his face suffused in a broad smile. As this was most

The Gaon Explained

rare, R' Moshe could not refrain from asking him the cause of his merriment.

R' Yehoshua Leib remembered his promise to R' Moshe and said, "I would not reveal this to any other person, but I am under an obligation and will tell you why I am smiling.

"As I was lying here, I envisioned a meeting of rabbis being held in my home. They sat about discussing a passage in the Vilna Gaon's commentary. Each one was explaining it as he understood it. I also offered my view on the true meaning of the Gaon's words. As we were arguing back and forth, one of the men present rose and said, 'The author is right here. Why don't we ask him directly?' The Gaon of Vilna clarified the words he had written and his explanation coincided exactly with what I had just said. At that moment I rose, looked at him and beamed with pleasure. And that is how you found me."

HE WAS ALSO STRICT with his disciples when it came to paying debts. One of his students was once walking along when an elderly

Care With Another's Money

Jew slipped and fell at his feet. The student called for some porters and had the man carried to the hospital. After they had done so, they went to the young man's house to demand their wages. Destitute, he explained that he had no money with which to pay them. Besides, he told them, they were just as obligated as he to help out a Jew in distress.

R' Yehoshua Leib learned of the incident and summoned the disciple to him. He informed him that he must pay the porters at once so as not to transgress the prohibition against postponing a laborer's payment. R' Yehoshua Leib gave him some money and told him to locate the porters. Finally, the student found them all and paid each for his labor, with a bonus in addition.

On another occasion, his disciples held a eulogy for R' Leib Chafetz, a man renowned for his zeal. At the end of the gathering, after the crowd had dispersed, R' Yehoshua Leib paid the *shammash* a coin for R' Leib's soul on behalf of all the people who had been present during the prayer. He had heard the *shammash* recite the formula "... for the entire congregation who pledge charity ..." and had felt obligated to make good that pledge so as not to bring that gathering of Jews to task for not having given charity.

CHAPTER EIGHT

His Righteousness

R' YEHOSHUA LEIB DISKIN'S SOUL was exalted beyond the rest of his contemporaries. Yet, when it was necessary, he knew how to descend to the people, to attune himself to the prayers and needs of his generation and to bear their burden and suffering.

People traveled to Jerusalem to meet him; they knocked at his door day and night; they elbowed their way into his tiny home to pour out their hearts before him. And afterwards, they would tell tales of miraculous succor. They regarded him as endowed with the power of conferring blessing.

His contemporaries used to say: From R' Yehoshua Leib's manner of expression and from his choice of words, one knew whether the ill person would recover or not.

Try as he might, he did not always succeed in camouflaging his powers. Some deeds were so great that they ripped away, as it were, his veil of secrecy.

R' YEHOSHUA LEIB WAS NEVER impressed upon hearing that doctors had despaired of a patient's life, even when the patient appeared

A Doctor Is Not Authorized to Despair
moribund. His faith went beyond mortal grasp. When people came to him saying that a patient's condition was hopeless, he would say, time and again, "And who authorized the doctor to despair?"

R' Yeshaya Cheshin's wife was stricken with cancer shortly after her marriage. Three of Jerusalem's most famous physicians concurred in their opinion that she had no chance of recovery. Their hopelessness aroused a general sorrow in the community for the afflicted woman was famous for her good works. Her condition was so critical that R' Yisrael Binyamin Lampert, the famous Jerusalem *maggid*, was called in to recite the *vidui* with the dying woman.

At this point, R' Yeshaya rushed over to R' Yehoshua Leib and poured out the bitterness in his heart. R' Yehoshua Leib reassured him, announcing emphatically, "She will recover." R' Yeshaya did not accept this at face value. He asked whether it might not help as a *segulah* (charm) to arrange a divorce (an accepted custom for such drastic situations). But R' Yehoshua Leib refused to hear of it. He said, "I was your matchmaker. G-d forbid that you divorce her. She will recover!"

This incident took place on a Friday. By the following Monday, the woman was out of bed. She lived for another fifty years.

R' NOTA GERSHON ROSENFELD became so ill in his youth that the doctors despaired of his recovery. One of his relatives went to R'

Why Bother?
Yehoshua Leib to ask him to pray for the youth. He calmly replied that the boy would recover, but the relative was not convinced and asked if they should not add another name. R' Yehoshua Leib repeated, "I said that he would recover, so why bother?"

Sure enough, R' Nota slowly recovered.

R' Shalom Eisenbach's son once became mortally ill. The mother was removed from the sickroom to spare her the sight of her son's death. She rushed to R' Yehoshua Leib to ask if they should change the child's name. "What is his name?" he asked. "Chaim Eliezer," she replied.

"In that case, there is no need to change it. He will recover."

And he did.

EARLY ONE FRIDAY MORNING, R' Shlomo Aharon Wertheimer ran to R' Yehoshua Leib to pray for his son Yaakov, who was hovering between life and death.

The Healing Shabbos

"Rest assured," said R' Yehoshua Leib. "*Shabbos* is itself a remedy."

That Friday evening there was a sudden improvement in the child's condition, which the doctors were at a loss to explain.

R' TZVI MICHEL SHAPIRA fathered numerous children who died in infancy. Over ten children passed away in rapid succession. In his desperation, he sent a letter to R' Yehoshua Leib who was then abroad, begging him to pray. He did so and R' Tzvi Michel was soon blessed with a son who survived infancy.

The Power of Prayer

R' David Tiktin, a confidant of R' Yehoshua Leib, once rushed into his master's house weeping hysterically. His young son was dying.

Rising from his seat, R' Yehoshua Leib reassured him, saying, "Heaven gives sooner than it takes back." R' David returned home to find that his son had weathered the crisis. It was not long before he recovered completely.

R' EPHRAIM EISENBERG, attendant of R' Yitzchak Winograd, had a daughter who developed an affliction in her feet. Her condition was so severe that doctors despaired of her life unless her feet were amputated.

Surgery Is Not the Best Solution

But R' Yehoshua Leib advised the anxious father not to amputate her legs. The father followed his advice, despite the doctor's insistence that only amputation offered any hope of saving the girl.

The girl recovered completely.

R' Zeidel Weisfish once pleaded with R' Yehoshua Leib to pray for his son's vision. For several days, the boy had been unable to open his eyes.

"Go home," said R' Yehoshua Leib reassuringly.

As soon as the father set foot in his house, the boy was able to open his eyes.

Before the Call . . .

SHEINDEL BLAU, A WELL-KNOWN woman of good works, used to tell the following story. One night, her oldest son, Moshe, suddenly took ill. As soon as day broke, she rushed off to R' Yehoshua Leib Diskin for help.

Before she had a chance to tell him what was troubling her, he calmed her, saying,"The child will recover."

Just as He Said

R' MOSHE WEINGARTEN'S twelve-year-old son, Chaim Hirsch, was ill. The distraught mother rushed to R' Yehoshua Leib to ask him to pray for the boy.

"Your son will recover and live to produce generations," he assured her.

The boy recuperated, matured and got married. After fathering two sons, he became ill and died at the age of twenty-two.

On the day he died, people recalled what R' Yehoshua Leib had said to his mother ten years before and marveled at the precision of his language. Indeed, Chaim Hirsch had produced two sons — generations — before dying.

The Taste of Tallow

WHEN R' YEHOSHUA LEIB was rav of Lomza, he was once visited by a poor young girl who poured out a tale of woe. She served as a maid in the homes of wealthy Jews but was emaciated and drawn. Everything she ate, she said, tasted like tallow fat and was repugnant to her. She had already visited many great doctors and traveled as far as Berlin in search of help but no one was able to cure her strange affliction. Meanwhile, she was growing thinner by the day and her strength was quickly ebbing.

R' Yehoshua Leib understood that this was no mere physical ailment but that it had deeper roots. He asked her to think back when she had begun feeling this way. She recalled how she had once worked for a rich but miserly Jew. A *treif* tallow candle once fell into a pot of food. She ran to tell her master and he told her not to reveal the incident to anyone. The girl had remained silent while the entire family ate from that forbidden dish. And from that time, she now realized, everything she ate tasted of tallow.

"You have been punished enough, already," said R' Yehoshua Leib. "You need suffer no longer for Hashem has forgiven you. Everything will be all right."

The maid breathed in relief. And from that day on she was free of her strange disease.

Good Counsel

WHEN PEOPLE CAME to R' Yehoshua Leib asking him to pray for a sick relative, he sometimes offered a brief prayer on the spot and at other times went on to give advice. Sometimes his counsel would be logical; at other times, it required faith. Whatever the case, his words invariably helped.

His instructions would be given tersely. Once he had spoken, he would offer no explanations nor add anything to what he had said.

A man once went mad. His family went to R' Yehoshua Leib to plead that he pray for him.

"Study *Mishnayos Zeraim* with the patient," was his advice.

Not questioning his words, the family began to study regularly with the sick man and slowly he improved until he recovered fully.

A woman once sought R' Yehoshua Leib's blessing: all her children, she wept, died in infancy.

He advised her to begin reciting *birkas hamazon* after meals from a prayerbook, rather than by heart. She followed his counsel and was soon blessed with children who survived infancy.

A man asked him to pray that his son, who lived in Russia, be blessed with children. R' Yehoshua Leib told him, "Your son should pick himself up from the mud."

The name of the region in which the son lived was synonymous to the Yiddish word for mud. Following his advice, the son moved away and was blessed with children.

R' Moshe Shochet became ill and was told by his doctor to go to Jaffa. Upon his return, he once again fell sick with the same illness and sent someone to ask R' Yehoshua Leib for advice.

R' Yehoshua Leib asked, "Did he go to the Western Wall upon his return from Jaffa? Let him visit it and he will recover."

R' Yisrael David Braverman, son of the saintly R' Zorach, contracted diphtheria as an infant and his life was in danger. It was shortly before sundown on a Friday when his mother gathered him up in her arms and rushed over to R' Yehoshua Leib who lived in the same courtyard. She wept hysterically that her son was dying.

He fed the infant a spoon of chicken soup. The boy's eyes lit up as he swallowed the soup and he felt better immediately.

R' DAVID BAHARAN TOLD the story of the time his son, R' Nachum, had a violent nosebleed on his way to his *yeshivah*, Ohel Moshe. At

An Unusual Calculation

that moment, R' Yehoshua Leib happened to look outside the window and saw R' Nachum bleeding profusely.

He opened the window and called out, "Go on to the *yeshivah*. Once you are inside, the blood will stop flowing."

R' Nachum continued on, entered the *beis medrash*, and amazingly his nose stopped bleeding.

R' Yehoshua Leib attempted to explain away his prediction as nothing more than a simple calculation: "I watched him walking slowly and noticed that the drops were growing smaller and further apart. At that rate, I calculated the nosebleed would cease altogether by the time he reached his destination!"

A MAN WAS INDUCTED into the army and taken far away to the front lines. Time passed and his wife received a letter from his

Found Alive

commanding officer that her husband had died.

On the basis of this letter, the wife applied to the *beis din* for permission to remarry. It was granted and before long she was engaged to a Chabad *chassid*.

The *chassid* went to his rebbe, the Tzemach Tzedek, for his permission and his blessing. But the Tzemach Tzedek refused unless the permission to remarry also carried R' Yehoshua Leib's sanction.

The woman went to him with her letter. Instead of accepting this evidence of her husband's death, he advised her to send a special messenger to the city where her husband had been stationed during his military service and check out his whereabouts. The messenger would have to stay over *Rosh Hashanah* and *Yom Kippur* to satisfy his specifications.

The woman did as she had been bid. The messenger met her still-living husband at the synagogue on *Yom Kippur*.

A JERUSALEM BUSINESSMAN became the object of gossip and slander. It grew so unbearable that he fled abroad, leaving his wife and children in Jerusalem, starving and helpless. He simply vanished, without leaving a trace. Years passed and nothing was heard of him.

Go to Paris

Once, R' Leib Salant, son of R' Shmuel, had to take a trip to Frankfurt. To his surprise, he met the man sitting up front by the eastern wall of the synagogue alongside the other dignitaries.

R' Leib accosted him on his way out and rebuked him for leaving a family without any means of support and for not having communicated with them. The man became alarmed that he would be publicly exposed and slipped R' Leib one hundred marks to deliver to his family. He assured him that he would follow soon thereafter.

R' Leib returned to Jerusalem with the good news. The family was overjoyed. They painted the house, repaired the furniture and awaited his arrival. They waited in vain. More years passed without any word. The *agunah* visited R' Shmuel Salant time and again and wept over her bitter fate. Now, in addition to her poverty, she was an object of shame and derision. She could no longer bear it.

R' Shmuel sent a letter to the rabbi of Frankfurt inquiring about the man. He received the reply that the man had resided there for some time but had left long ago for France. This letter only intensified the woman's feeling of helplessness and abandonment. The family was crushed.

The *agunah* came to R' Yehoshua Leib and poured out all the bitterness in her heart. She begged him to do all in his power to help her.

R' Yehoshua Leib calmed the distraught woman. "If he said he was going to France, he probably did so. And where in France would one go? To Paris, of course. He must be there," he told her.

"So what?" she said bitterly.

"I suggest that you go to Paris at once."

"But I cannot afford the fare!" she murmured.

"The community committee will lay out the money for your traveling expenses," he reassured her.

The woman went at once to the central committee to ask for travel expenses to Paris. The trustees informed her that such a large allocation required the approval of R' Shmuel Salant. She continued on to R' Shmuel Salant and told him what R' Yehoshua Leib had advised.

R' Shmuel's family were surprised at the suggestion. They considered the evidence upon which the community was being asked to allocate the money too flimsy. Who could even tell whether the man had been telling the truth when he said he was going to France or whether he had just been covering his tracks? And even if he had gone to France, who could say he had gone to Paris? They found it hard to believe that R' Yehoshua Leib would expect the central committee to approve such a large outlay for such a doubtful venture.

But the woman would not let up. She wailed and moaned until she wore everyone out. R' Feivel Hirschberg, *shammash* of the *beis din*, was sent to R' Yehoshua Leib to hear exactly what he had told the woman. R' Yehoshua Leib, true to his usual style, repeated verbatim what he had said to the woman, "Since the man said he was going to France, one can assume that he did go there. And if to France, he certainly went to Paris."

"I am sure," he added, "that the central committee will assume the burden of her traveling expenses."

R' Shmuel Salant approved the allocation and that day, the full amount was given to the woman and she left for Paris.

Upon her arrival, she made arrangements to stay at the communal hostel, the *hachnasas orchim* house, and then began her search.

Some time passed and the woman sensed heightened activity in one of the large rooms of the house. She was told that a wedding was to take place that day and that the residents were invited to partake. That afternoon, the place began filling up with guests.

The *chassan* sat up front, dressed in new clothing from top to toe. The guests had all gathered and were awaiting the rav's arrival to begin the ceremony. The woman looked up at the *chassan* and got the shock of her life. He was none other than her long-lost husband!

She was so overwrought that she fell down in a faint. She was carried out and revived. At that moment, the *chassan* came over to her and whispered something in her ear. The *chupah* was postponed. The man and his true wife slipped out a side door, unnoticed, and left the city. They, eventually, returned to Jerusalem, to everyone's great surprise.

A YEMENITE JEW LIVING in Jerusalem used to supply clay to R' Yehoshua Leib each year at *Pesach* time for a new oven. He was

Lifesaving Counsel
careful to deliver the clay in new sacks which had never been used for flour or come in contact with *chametz*.

One year, the Yemenite came to the *rebbetzin* to receive the new sacks. It was early in *Nissan*, when Arab workers dug for clay outside the city to provide Jewish households with clay for new ovens or the repair of old ones. While he stood in the courtyard, waiting for her to bring the sacks, R' Yehoshua Leib called him over. "I don't advise you to go digging there, today," he said.

The man seemed to hesitate, weighing the advice in his mind. R' Yehoshua Leib, then, promised to pay him a full day's wage if he spent that day sitting in the *yeshivah*, reciting *Tehillim*.

The Yemenite agreed and said *Tehillim* all day.

The following day, news reached the city that there had been an avalanche at the clay pits. An entire mountainside had collapsed, burying alive several of the Arabs who had been digging there, together with their donkeys.

R' ZORACH BRAVERMAN of Jerusalem once won a lottery for an apartment in the Strauss complex on the way to Damascus Gate. He

**Silence —
Out of Love**

went to ask R' Yehoshua Leib whether to move there or not, but he ignored the question.

Time passed and the matter became urgent. If he did not move into the apartment, R' Zorach would forfeit his right to it. He approached R' Yehoshua Leib again, but still received no response of any kind.

Realizing that no answer was in itself an answer, he decided to remain where he was and forego his right. Someone else was awarded the apartment.

Time passed and a terrible tragedy took place in the compound. A huge stone in the floor, covering up the water cistern in the cellar below, became dislodged and the stone, together with an infant, plummeted down into the cistern.

AT THE BEGINNING OF R' Yehoshua Leib's rabbinical career, when he had just come to Lomza, a Jewish businessman went bankrupt and

**A Successful
Chatterer**

was arraigned by the authorities.

At that time, there also lived in Lomza a chicken and egg dealer who supplied many officials in the city, including the mayor. She was an inveterate chatterbox.

One morning, when the woman came to deliver her order of eggs to the mayor, the mayor's wife did not give her her customary greeting. Surprised, she inquired why, and was told that the mayor's son was critically ill. "I knew it! I knew it!"she exclaimed volubly, "I heard it from our rabbi. I also heard it said that the mayor brought it on, himself. If he were to exonerate the Jew in his custody, his son would get better."

When he learned what she had said, the mayor called the woman to his study to confirm the report. She was thunderstruck, for she had fabricated the story on the spur of the moment and had never heard the rabbi say anything of the sort. But what could she do now? Admit that she had let her imagination run wild? She did not have the courage to do that and stuck to her story.

She left the mayor's house very frightened and went directly to R' Yehoshua Leib's *beis medrash*. She burst into tears and confessed her sin, which had put him in a delicate and dangerous situation.

He calmed her with a short statement, "Salvation is the Almighty's." That evening, the mayor sent a special messenger to verify whether the woman's tale was true. R' Yehoshua Leib replied, "Free the prisoner and your son will recover." And so it was.

DURING THE PERIOD THAT R' Yehoshua Leib served as rav of Lomza, an elderly scholar denied a teaching of our Sages. As it is

Midah K'Neged Midah

known, the Song of the Sea which the Israelites uttered upon seeing their enemy drowned in the Red Sea is written in poetic form in the Torah scroll, spaced and staggered, like bricks in a wall. This man maintained that the verse, "For the horse of Pharaoh, with chariot and horsemen, entered the water and Hashem brought upon them the waters of the sea," should be written normally, since it is a summation and not part of the song.

When R' Yehoshua Leib heard this, he was appalled. He sent a message to the elderly man demanding that he not repeat his remarks, which were at variance with the teachings of our Sages. The man scoffed at the young rav's warning and persisted. R' Yehoshua Leib sent him another message, threatening that he would be punished if he continued to publicize his opinion.

Some time passed. One Friday, the elderly man went to immerse himself in the *mikveh* before *Shabbos*. He fainted in the water and drowned.

This event made a strong impression throughout the city, since many people felt that the drastic punishment exactly fit the man's sin. It was a realization of the very verse of which he had contested the traditional writing: "And Hashem brought upon them the waters . . ."

WHILE R' YEHOSHUA LEIB WAS serving in Lomza, two men brought a case to his brother, R' Avraham Shmuel Diskin, whose decision was

An Accurate Assumption

not acceptable to the parties. They decided to take the matter up with a different *dayan* and chose one of the sages of Brisk.

They traveled to Brisk and they laid their case before the rav there, without telling him that they had already been judged by a different rav.

The second decision did not fully coincide with R' Avraham Shmuel's ruling. The two men decided to stir up a scandal at the expense of R' Avraham Shmuel, and the matter became the talk of the day. When R' Avraham Shmuel saw that he had lost all stature in the public eye, he turned to his older brother for help. He described the case as it had first been presented to him.

R' Yehoshua Leib agreed with him and wrote a long letter to the rav in Brisk, who had differed slightly in his own ruling:

"In my opinion, my brother ruled correctly. One cannot imagine that a man of his stature would err, and besides, 'G-d stands in the council of judges.' We can therefore infer that there was trickery in the presentation of the facts. I venture to say that the two men connived between them and presented the case before the rav in such a way as to put it in a false perspective. In such an instance, where the foundation is false to begin with, a gross error can arise, since the rule that no stumbling block emerges from a true court of Torah no longer applies. A true judgment could not possibly have resulted, being built on falsehood. This, then, is the reason for the error in the decision."

Upon investigation it was discovered that the two men had actually switched roles and each taken the other's position before the second *beis din*. R' Yehoshua Leib's intuitiveness had turned out to be the truth.

THE AUTHOR OF *CHEVEL YAAKOV*, a disciple of R' Yehoshua Leib's in Shklov, used to tell how the mayor of a certain Russian city vented
Cherem all of his hatred upon his Jewish citizens. He made life miserable for them through a wide array of harsh, oppressive decrees.

The Jewish populace buckled under his yoke and came to R' Yehoshua Leib with their woes. He quietly asked those close to him to find out the name of the mayor's mother and give him the information.

R' Yehoshua Leib secretly organized a small *minyan* including his disciple, author of *Chevel Yaakov*. One midnight, they descended to a pitch-black subterranean cellar. They blew *shofar*s into barrels to muffle the sound and placed the mayor into *cherem*. He died shortly thereafter.

IN 5658 (1898), R' YITZCHAK YERUCHAM, R' Yehoshua Leib's only son, who was living abroad, was about to marry off his daughter. He

The Unheeded Hint

wrote to his father requesting a blessing for the new couple.

In his last letter ever, R' Yehoshua Leib hinted that his son should bring his daughter to Jerusalem to receive his blessing in person before the wedding.

R' Yitzchak Yerucham did not take the hint. The short time still left until the wedding would not have permitted such a lengthy voyage. The wedding took place, as scheduled, in Vilna, on *Rosh Chodesh Shevat* and was attended by great rabbinical figures near and far. R' Chaim Ozer Grodzenski officiated.

On that very day, a telegram arrived in Oman, where R' Yitzchak Yerucham lived, informing him of his father's passing in Jerusalem. The news reached Vilna shortly before the *chupah*, but R' Yitzchak Yerucham was only told of it by hint. "Return to Oman," was the message. He left the wedding in the midst of the festivities and returned home.

When he entered his room and read the telegram on the table, he burst into tears.

After a long time, he recovered. His first words were, "I wondered why father hinted that I should visit him together with my daughter right before the wedding. Now I know why. His vision was far seeing, but now it is too late."

R' TZVI MICHEL SHAPIRA of Jerusalem once visited R' Yehoshua Leib in his home at a time when R' Eliyahu Strelitzer of Eishishok was

"A Time to Give Birth"

there. R' Yehoshua Leib suddenly turned to them and said, "R' Eliyahu, you have a wonderful daughter while you, R' Tzvi Michel, have a fine son. I think it a good idea for them to get married."

R' Eliyahu demurred, "But my daughter is only fifteen years old. If she were to get married now, she would be a mother at the age of sixteen.

That is too young, I think." To which R' Yehoshua Leib commented, "Who says that it will turn out that way? She may only become a mother in a few years."

His suggestion was accepted by both sides and soon the engagement was celebrated. R' Tzvi Michel's son was betrothed to R' Eliyahu's daughter, Chaya Leah, and the wedding was set for *Nissan* 5650 (1890).

Chaya Leah did not give birth to her first child until four years had passed.

R' ZALMAN ZWEIG OF JERUSALEM once told of two young American tourists who went to pay their respects to R' Yehoshua Leib, but were

Their Bite Is Like Fire

in a light-headed frame of mind.

He told them, among other things, of the importance of the Diskin orphanage, which he had recently founded. The orphanage was still so new that it had not yet won a name for itself and at the mention of it, they could not help chuckling disrespectfully and joking about it. R' Yehoshua Leib listened and reacted violently, berating them for making fun of orphans. He fixed them with his burning gaze and stalked out of the room.

The two young men returned to America and shortly thereafter both died.

R' Yehoshua Leib was once told of a Jerusalem family who enrolled a son in a secular school in defiance of the ban. He said, "Him? Who knows what will become of him?" His casual remark was borne out. During the First World War, the head of the family traveled to Damascus and was never heard of again.

THE TRUSTEES OF A *KOLLEL* once bought a large property near the Damascus Gate for the establishment of a hospital. When they came to

A *Tzaddik's* Utterance

R' Yehoshua Leib to tell him about it, he said, "May it be the Almighty's will that the *Shechinah* not rest upon your endeavor." He meant that there should be no sick people, as the *Gemara* says, "The *Shechinah* rests upon the head of a sick man" (*Shabbos* 12).

R' Yehoshua Leib's literal meaning was also fulfilled. The sale fell through and the land was not purchased. Later, a different plot was bought in the New City, in west Jerusalem, upon which the old Shaarei Zedek Hospital stood for many decades.

The Accuser Accused

WHENEVER TWO PEOPLE CAME before R' Yehoshua Leib's court, they would present their cases to the judges. The judges would then enter his room to discuss the case before arriving at a decision. R' Yehoshua Leib never saw the faces of the litigants.

A man and wife once came before the court with a claim against a third person who had allegedly besmirched the woman's good name. R' Yehoshua Leib told his wife to take the woman aside and she did.

When she entered, he raised his voice and berated her for having dared come to the court when she knew the accusation against her was true. The woman was taken aback by this sudden attack. She bowed her head and admitted her guilt.

R' Yehoshua Leib left the room and entered the courtroom. The husband was still presenting his side of the story before the judges. R' Yehoshua Leib turned to him and said, "The case has already been decided. Go and divorce your wife."

Help From Heaven

WHILE SERVING AS RAV of Lomza, R' Yehoshua Leib was surrounded by a number of young men who had already studied *halachah* but needed practical experience. Any question brought to him was first presented to them.

An animal's lung of questionable halachic status was once brought before the rav. The young students studied the problem in *Poskim*. They found that the Shach prohibited it. But when the question came before R' Yehoshua Leib, he said the animal was permissible. Surprised, the young men showed him the text of the Shach. "There is a mistake in the text of the Shach," he said.

They were alarmed. "When such a question comes before an expert like you, you automatically know what to rule and can even overrule a mistake in the text of the Shach. But when such a question comes before novices like us, what are we to do? How were we to know that the text of the Shach was not accurate? How, then, can we ever assume the responsibility of the rabbinate?"

"You must try your utmost," he reassured them. "If a young rabbi studies to his full capacity and has the greater glory of the Almighty at heart, no harm will arise from his rulings. Heaven will guide him to do the right thing."

Just at that moment, R' Yehoshua Leib happened to glance out the window and saw R' Yosef Chaver coming to him. He said to his disciples, "Now is your chance to prove the truth of what I just told you. The Yadvebner Rav, a great *tzaddik*, is coming up the walk. Lead him into another room and present this very question to him."

The guest entered and asked them, "What were you discussing just now?" The young rabbis showed them the lung and asked his opinion. He pronounced it kosher. "But according to the Shach," they said, showing it to him in the text, "the animal is *treif*." He was thoughtful and murmured, "Hmmm. According to this, I must have made a mistake.'

He studied the Shach again, analyzing each word. The Brisker Rav then entered the room and greeted him. Seeing him engrossed in study, R' Yehoshua Leib said to his disciples, "What happened?"

They told him. The Brisker Rav smiled, "Didn't I tell you? A rav who is genuinely seeking the truth and who is truly G-d-fearing will intuitively know the correct answer, for Heaven guides him."

A COUPLE ONCE CAME TO the Brisker Rav for a divorce. The scribe was in the midst of writing the *get*, when R' Yehoshua Leib stopped

The Dog Gave It Away
him and postponed the divorce for a later date. Those present wondered why he had done so. This had never happened before.

The following day, the reason for the delay became clear. The woman had come with a man who was not her husband in order to procure a false divorce.

R' Yehoshua Leib, true to form, had a simple explanation for the matter. "There was no miracle of any sort," he said, "but simple logic. I noticed the two people walking with a dog. The dog kept going from one to the other. I thought to myself, 'If this were an estranged couple, why would the dog be going from one to the other? A dog is used to following one close to him. I concluded that these two were not man and wife, that they were not quarreling with one another and were not even married. And you see, my instinct was right."

A JERUSALEM JEW HAD a profligate son who defied his parents at every turn and disgraced the family name with his deeds. The father's

The Fragrance of Torah

friends strongly suggested that since the boy was a disruptive factor at school and a bad example to the other children, he might as well transfer him to a secular school where he would do less damage.

Being a devout man, the father refused to hear of it. When he could no longer stand up under the constant barrage of advice, he went to R' Yehoshua Leib with his problem.

R' Yehoshua Leib told him not to do a thing. "Let your son continue in *cheder*. Even if he does not absorb any knowledge, at least he is in a Torah environment and benefits from the fragrance of Torah." He told him to continue praying and, with the help of Hashem, he would eventually reap *nachas* (parental satisfaction).

The son grew into a G-d-fearing, observant Jew.

R' YEHOSHUA LEIB'S WIFE once complained to R' Moshe Jules, one of his closest acquaintances, that her husband had stopped eating the

Tzaddikim Are Protected From Error

chicken she served him each day. "He only eats the soup, but this is not nourishing enough. He will become weak," she said.

R' Moshe was known for his practicality and good sense. He advised her to serve the main course before the soup. That way, he would at least eat the chicken, which was more important for his health.

This idea seemed sound. The following day, the *rebbetzin* did just that. She laid a portion of chicken before R' Yehoshua Leib. But, when he noticed a break in the bone, which posed a halachic question, he refused to touch the food.

When he questioned his wife as to why she had decided to forego the soup that day, he learned that it had been R' Moshe Jules' idea.

This information pleased him greatly. He saw in it the Hand of Providence preventing him from eating forbidden food. Had his wife first served the chicken soup, he would have eaten it without realizing that there was a problem with the chicken.

A similar incident once happened to R' Yosef Dov Ber Soloveitchik. He was traveling from Warsaw to Slutzk and stopped over in Brisk to visit R' Yehoshua Leib. It was two days before *Yom Kippur*. R' Yehoshua Leib was overjoyed to see him for the two enjoyed a warm regard for one another. Whenever they met, one would recite the *shehechiyanu* blessing while the other replied, "*Amen*." When R' Yosef Dov Ber was about to leave, his host ordered provisions packed for the way. The *rebbetzin* prepared half a chicken, which he took along. He intended to spend *Yom Kippur* in Breze.

On *erev Yom Kippur*, R' Yosef Dov Ber sat down to eat the chicken. When he eyed it on his plate, he refused to touch it, claiming that it was not fresh. His companion, R' Shaul Wolfson from Slutzk, smelled the chicken and said that it seemed all right to him. But, R' Yosef Dov Ber adamantly refused to touch it.

Meanwhile, a telegram arrived from R' Yehoshua Leib informing R' Yosef Dov Ber that the chicken was not kosher and that he should throw it away.

Prior to sending the telegram, R' Yehoshua Leib had said to his family, "I am confident that R' Yosef Ber will not eat the chicken, and thus, there is no question of him sinning even unwittingly. I am sending the telegram, nevertheless, since this is what the *halachah* requires of me, though I deem it superfluous."

R' Yehoshua Leib once took ill on *erev Yom Kippur*. His disciples feared that the fast would be too much for him and sent for Dr. Mazreika, a Greek medical expert, to determine what he must do.

The doctor was not familiar with Yiddish and brought along an interpreter, but R' Yehoshua Leib refused to rely on him. The *rebbetzin*, who knew some Greek, was asked to be present at the examination.

The *rebbetzin* was then in the midst of the *erev Yom Kippur Shemoneh Esrei*, which is a long prayer and said with deep concentration. R' Yehoshua Leib asked the doctor to wait until she finished and he complied. He waited and waited. Seeing that there was no end to his waiting, the doctor picked himself up and left.

In the end, R' Yehoshua Leib fasted that year. After the fast was over and no harm had come to him, he joyfully said that it had been contrived by Heaven that he would fast the entire day.

A FLOUR MERCHANT ONCE LOST a large sum of money. He raised a furor over the lost money; the entire city knew of his loss. Though he searched high and low for it, there was no trace of the money.

Returning Lost Property

Depressed and beside himself with worry, he went to R' Yehoshua Leib who assured him that *Hashem* would replenish his loss. His choice of words comforted the man. Late that night, an elderly woman knocked on his door carrying the small purse containing the missing money. The woman explained that she had struggled with her conscience whether to keep the purse she had found or return it to its owner. She had gone to bed that night, but had a fit of terror and could not sleep. In the end, she had decided to come and return the money.

WHEN THE RAV OF KOBRIN passed away, R' Yehoshua Leib, who was then in Brisk, traveled to the funeral together with the renowned R' Shalom Menashe.

The Heat of Torah

They traveled all night. The cold intensified towards morning and R' Shalom Menashe snuggled into his fur coat in an attempt to warm up. "Why are you shivering?" R' Yehoshua Leib asked him. "Because it's cold!" R' Shalom Menashe replied. "How can one be cold reviewing *Gemara* with *Tosafos*?" countered R' Yehoshua Leib in surprise.

R' YEHOSHUA LEIB USED TO use water drawn from the natural spring in Motza each year for his *matzah*-baking. Once, on the thirteenth of Nissan, R' Yosef Ralbag and another person close to R' Yehoshua Leib went to Motza to fetch the special well water. Upon their arrival, they met some Arabs who refused to let them approach the well.

He Performs the Will of His Devout

They were deeply distressed, for this was their last chance to draw the water. The sun was about to set; soon it would be too late. It was inconceivable that R' Yehoshua Leib would be without *matzos* that year! What could they do?

Consumed with hopelessness and sorrow, they sat down upon a large stone nearby and began weeping. Just then, a Turkish mounted policeman passed by. He stopped and asked them why they were weeping.

R' Yosef Ralbag explained as best he could. "Come with me," the policeman said, "I'll take care of everything." He led them to the well. At the sight of the armed policeman, the Arabs fled in terror. The two men drew the water under the protective eye of the Turkish policeman. When they had finished, they thanked him, but murmured their fears that the Arabs would return to molest them on the way home. The policeman agreed to accompany them all the way to the entrance of the city. To their relief, the water was delivered safely to R' Yehoshua Leib's house.

R' BINYAMIN DISKIN, R' Yehoshua Leib's father, is buried in a special tomb in the Lomza cemetery. Several years after his death, the

Let the Son Visit His Father

government sealed up that cemetery, as there was no more room for additional graves. The communal trustees established another burial area for the congregation.

R' Noach Yitzchak Diskin once came to pray at his father's grave and found one of the walls of the structure above it on the verge of collapse. He wrote to his brother, R' Yehoshua Leib, in Jerusalem, asking whether or not to repair it.

To his astonishment, R' Yehoshua Leib answered all the points in the letter except for this crucial one. R' Noach Yitzchak wrote to him again, and was even more surprised when again he ignored the question.

He complained to his relatives about the matter. Years passed, and the wall remained in disrepair, but it did not collapse, as had been expected.

Then R' Noach Yitzchak became ill and departed this world. The members of the *chevrah kadisha* (burial society) had just finished preparing his body for burial when the watchman at the cemetery came to tell them that one of the walls above R' Binyamin's grave had caved in that very night.

R' Yitzchak Bilkovsky, a relative of the *rebbetzin* with connections in high places, approached the mayor and asked for special permission to bury R' Noach Yitzchak next to his father, even though the cemetery had been closed for forty years. He noted that one wall of the mausoleum above the grave had just collapsed, leaving just enough room for an additional grave. The mayor looked into the matter and finally issued a special permit to bury R' Noach Yitzchak next to his father.

The Jews of Lomza now understood why R' Yehoshua Leib had never replied to his brother's question. He had had a good reason.

And They Shall Fear You

DURING THE TWENTY YEARS that he lived in Jerusalem, R' Yehoshua Leib could be seen each day walking through the alleys of the Old City. It was wondrous how the Arabs would rise to their full height, each time, and make way for him to pass.

Lime Logic

AS A YOUNG MAN, R' Zorach Braverman opened a small dye shop. But his customers used to complain that his dyes were not well absorbed into the clothing and faded quickly. On the other hand, clothing dyed by his Arab competitors kept their vivid colors much longer.

R' Zorach's expert tried valiantly to emulate them but he could not learn the secret of their ingredients. He, finally, approached an Arab craftsman and begged him to divulge the secret. The Arab was willing, but only for the huge fee of twenty-five napoleons (the coin of the realm). This was far too high a price for R' Zorach, even if he had not feared that the Arab would cheat him.

R' Zorach's Jewish expert kept an eye on his Arab competitors and tried to duplicate their dye. He noticed that they bought unusually large quantities of lime, which they apparently mixed with their dyes.

He experimented with lime, himself, but only succeeded in spoiling the dye and incurring great losses.

R' Zorach happened to mention his problem to R' Yehoshua Leib. The latter thought the problem through and came to a logical conclusion: if R' Zorach's expert saw the Arabs buying large quantities of lime, this must be good for dying. But, apparently, mixing was not the proper way. What seemed probable was to take the lime, fill a thick sack with it, seal it tight and then dip the entire sack into the dye.

When R' Zorach's expert tried this, he saw that this was the solution. His Arab competitors wondered how he had discovered the secret.

R' YEHOSHUA LEIB ONCE TOLD his disciple, R' Yaakov Orenstein, that whenever he was in doubt and had to check a source, he would **Help From Heaven** invariably open the right *sefer* to the right place.

R' HENOCH EISENSTADT from Greibe was negotiating with a flour dealer from Lomza over wheat for *matzos*. The dealer promised to **The Almighty** do him a favor and deliver the wheat to Greibe. **Will Repay** But along the way, a sudden downpour wet the entire batch of wheat, ruining it for *matzah*-baking.

R' Henoch refused to accept the shipment. He claimed that he had bought wheat for *matzos*, not wheat unfit for that purpose. The seller argued that he had sold kosher wheat of the highest caliber. When the rain wet it, it already belonged to the buyer and had been ruined when it was already in R' Henoch's possession.

The two men could not reach an agreement and went to the rav of Lomza for a ruling. R' Yehoshua Leib agreed with the seller. The transaction had already been completed prior to delivery to R' Henoch and the wheat had transferred to the hands of the buyer when it was rained on.

R' Henoch was miserable; he had incurred a terrible loss. How would he ever recoup his money? Seeing his chagrin, R' Yehoshua

Leib beckoned to him and said, "I am really sorry for you, but I trust that the Almighty will make good your loss."

R' Henoch was reassured. He took the shipment of wheat and stored it away in his cellar. That summer was a dry one. The country suffered from drought and the price of wheat shot up. R' Henoch sold his stock and received the price of *Pesach* wheat, which is much higher than regular wheat. All in all, he had incurred no loss, just as R' Yehoshua Leib had promised.

RIGHT BEFORE THE FIRST WORLD WAR, R' Yitzchak Yerucham Diskin emptied out the cash reserves of the Diskin Orphanage and

The Dream Visitor

bought a large amount of wheat. He told no one except for those closest to him, who could not understand why he had done so.

When war broke out, wheat became the most crucial commodity. People marveled at R' Yitzchak Yerucham's far-sightedness. Even the Turkish police had to resort to buying wheat from the orphanage's cellar.

R' Yitzchak Yerucham later explained that his father had appeared to him in a dream and ordered him to do just that. In his deep concern for the orphans, even in the Hereafter, R' Yehoshua Leib had made sure that they would not suffer hunger during the war.

A *MASKIL* ONCE CAME TO R' Yehoshua Leib while he was yet in Shklov, asking for a recommendation for a book he was publishing on

The Hoped-For Recommendation

the sanctification of the new moon. He knew that if the prestigious rav of Shklov gave his approval to the book, it would open up all doors for him.

R' Yehoshua Leib generally had nothing to do with *maskilim*. He loathed them with all his heart. Naturally, he had no intention of giving his approbation on the book. But he did not say so outright to the supplicant and remained silent when the man left his book behind so that he could leaf through it at his convenience.

When he returned the next day, R' Yehoshua Leib asked him to step inside the *beis din* chambers. The *maskil* happily complied, assured that he would received his hoped-for recommendation.

R' Yehoshua Leib leafed through his book and showed the author eighteen mistakes which he had found upon perusal. The *maskil* was an expert in the field of astronomy and was astounded at the expertise R' Yehoshua Leib exhibited in this area. He thought about his comments and conceded many of the points, though he tried to argue his way through the rest, claiming that he had copied from other reference works on the subject, which were probably not written clearly.

"An author who copies over facts from other sources without checking their validity does not deserve a recommendation," said R' Yehoshua Leib and sent him away empty-handed.

THE BRISKER RAV OCCASIONALLY took a stroll outdoors, accompanied by some of his disciples. He had special reasons for doing so, and

A Walk With R' Yosef Chaim Sonnenfeld

his conversation during these excursions was most enlightening for his companions.

One Friday afternoon, he stepped out with his disciple, R' Yaakov Gellis, when, suddenly, they met up with R' Yosef Chaim Sonnenfeld. He drew near and bowed his head before R' Yehoshua Leib and begged to be blessed. R' Yehoshua Leib laid both his hands upon his head and blessed him.

After they had continued some way, he noticed how surprised R' Yaakov was at that chance encounter and explained, "Whenever R' Yosef Chaim is confronted with a problem, be it a communal matter or family trouble such as illness, or even when he is puzzled by a difficult topic in his studies, he comes to me for a blessing. He thinks, apparently, that everything will be smoothed out. Now, too, something must be troubling him, or he would not have come seeking my blessing."

Once, when R' Yosef Chaim became seriously ill, R' Yehoshua Leib ordered that he be given the additional name of Yosef to his given name Chaim, saying, "May *Hashem* add on [*yosef*] more years of life." Only a few days later, he passed the crisis and was already on his way to recovery.

One *Purim*, R' Yosef Chaim came to R' Yehoshua Leib early in the morning bearing his *shalach manos*. R' Yehoshua Leib commended him for his promptness and alertness.

R' Yosef Chaim smiled and said, "I received my alacrity from you, my master. When you added the name Yosef to Chaim, you transformed the numerical value of my name to that of *zariz*, nimble and quick."

R' Yosef Chaim used to fast during the entire week of the Ten Days of Penitence. Once, when he visited R' Yehoshua Leib during this period, his master saw on his face that he was fasting. He challenged him outright, just to make sure. R' Yosef Chaim was so in awe that he could not reply, which R' Yehoshua Leib understood to be confirmation of his suspicions. He called out to the *rebbetzin* and said, "Bring a glass of tea and some cake for R' Yosef Chaim."

When she brought in the tray, the Brisker Rav ordered him to eat and drink. "It is not right for a Torah scholar to mortify himself," he said.

From that time on, whenever he fasted, R' Yosef Chaim made sure not to refrain from eating a full day, but to break the fast before night, so as not to act contrary to his master's will.

R' Yosef Chaim's wife once became critically ill. The best doctors were summoned but they could not cure her. R' Yosef Chaim dispatched a messenger to the Brisker Rav, begging him to pray for her. R' Yehoshua Leib sent back two napoleons and ordered that he bring the greatest experts to examine her. And he said upon that occasion, "Since you already resorted to natural channels, by consulting doctors, you must carry on and do your utmost in that direction."

A MAN ONCE CAME TO R' Yehoshua Leib asking if he should join the newly founded Achva (Brotherhood) organization whose purpose was

A Strong Affection

to unite all Jews in love and mutual self-help. He asked if was this not a form of observing the commandment of "Love your neighbor as yourself."

"That organization is laboring under a strong misconception," R' Yehoshua Leib answered. "There is no application of brotherly love here but of self-love. Whatever a person does for his fellow member is only so that he, in turn, will pay back the favor. And this is completely contrary to the Torah! We are commanded to love every Jew, even those who are not members of a fraternity. Furthermore, the Torah commands us to love our enemies, too. We are forbidden to bear grudges or avenge ourselves; rather, we are supposed to come to the aid of our enemies. Thus, joining such an organization is strictly against the Torah."

CHAPTER NINE

His Amazing Powers

R' YOSHE STERN, the pharmacist, once received a letter from a relative in Hungary asking his advice about a complex business matter. Not wishing to rely on his own opinion, **Word Count** R' Yoshe went to ask R' Yehoshua Leib's advice. He handed the letter, written closely together and filling both sides of the page, to R' Yehoshua Leib and waited for an answer.

He glanced casually at the letter and gave his opinion.

R' Yoshe left his house with the impression that he had not grasped the matter fully and returned to ask his advice a second time. "Did the rav read the entire letter?" he asked querulously.

R' Yehoshua Leib countered with the same question, "And did you read the letter? Can you tell me how many words it contains?"

R' Yoshe was silent. R' Yehoshua Leib continued, "Rest assured that I *did* read it." And he proceeded to tell R' Yoshe how many words were in the letter.

R' Yoshe returned home and painstakingly counted up the words on both sides. R' Yehoshua Leib's count had been perfectly accurate!

DURING HIS LAST DAYS ON EARTH, an event occurred which startled the entire city and became the talk of Jerusalem for a long time.

The Number of Threads

R' Yaakov Orenstein, an eyewitness to the scene, related:

Let me tell you what my own eyes saw in his last week. A woman brought a stain for R' Yehoshua Leib to examine. With a brief glance, he ruled it unclean. On the following day she returned with another stain. He studied it for an instant and said, "But is this not the very sample you showed me yesterday and which I said was unclean?"

"No," she insisted. "This is a different one."

"Why don't you admit the truth?" he asked. "I say that this is the very one you showed me yesterday. If you want, I can tell you how many threads the swatch of material had in its length and breadth." And he gave a number.

I counted the threads, along with a friend, and found the number of threads in its warp and woof to be exactly as R' Yehoshua Leib had said. Upon hearing his proof, the woman quoted in awe, " 'Indeed, there is a G-d in this place, and I did not know it.' Someone told me to bring it a second time. Please forgive me for testing you."

R' YAAKOV ORENSTEIN used to say that R' Yehoshua Leib never had to leaf through a *sefer* to find what he was looking for. He recognized

The Glory of a Page

each page according to its individual character, or as he put it, its particular glory and grandeur. From a mere glance, he would jab his finger directly at a spot and find what he was seeking.

THE MAGNITUDE OF HIS GRASP enabled him to get the gist of an entire *sefer* merely by leafing through it. While serving in Kovno, he

The Magnitude of His Grasp

was once visited by R' Yosef Dov Ber Soloveitchik. R' Yehoshua Leib asked him to share some of his *chiddushim*. R' Yosef Dov

Ber complied with two or three concepts he had developed, in different areas. Then R' Yehoshua Leib asked him for his explanation of a different problem. As he was about to give his response, R' Yehoshua Leib predicted precisely what he was going to say.

When the works of R' Akiva Eiger first appeared, R' Yehoshua Leib asked his students to tell him some of the contents. They would ask R' Akiva Eiger's question and he would counter with the printed reply, saying, "This is probably what R' Akiva Eiger would say." And each time, he would accurately guess what that sage had written.

The author of *Chevel Yaakov*, a disciple of R' Yehoshua Leib in Shklov, was sitting in his master's house one Friday, looking through a copy of *Chemdas Tzvi*, which lay on the table. R' Yehoshua Leib walked in and asked him what he was studying. The disciple reviewed some of the *chiddushim* it contained. R' Yehoshua Leib immediately grasped the style and continued on his own, quoting, with uncanny accuracy, what was written in that work, without having seen it himself!

R' Meir Simcha used to say of this incident, "Doubtless, his phenomenal grasp is mind-boggling, but even more remarkable is his piety. When he saw that he had lost the train of the author's thought, he felt it necessary to reinforce his mind's potency through an act of charity."

WHILE STILL IN LOMZA, R' Yehoshua Leib was visited by the city's scholars during a festival. They came in pairs to wish him, "*Gut Yom Tov*," and receive his blessing in return. They

In One Breath streamed before him, men from near and far, one pair entering and the other leaving. To each, he said a *chiddush*. When the pairs later compared notes, they learned that each of those *chiddushim* had revolved around one statement in *Tosafos*, but that each was totally different from the other.

R' ARYE LEIB FRUMKIN WRITES, "I was once telling R' Yehoshua Leib about the new methods which had been developed in grape cultivation

It Contains All as presented in a certain work in German. To my surprise, he already knew about most of these methods and showed them to me in a commentary by the Rash

M'Shantz and the Yerushalmi on *Shevi'is*. In addition, he proposed several of his own ideas for improvements in wine cultivation."

A WOMAN ONCE CAME to R' Yehoshua Leib asking if it was worthwhile slaughtering a chicken infested with lice. Those present

Why the Lice burst into laughter, until he pronounced that such a bird must be *treif*.

When he saw their surprise, he turned to them and said, "Why do you think the lice attacked this bird more than others? All peck together in one farmyard. The answer is that chickens habitually throw back their heads and shake off the lice. But a chicken with a broken shoulder bone cannot do so, and remains infested with them."

R' YEHOSHUA LEIB WAS ENDOWED with amazing physical strengths. To the last moment, his hearing and vision were acutely attuned. He

His Physical Powers never wore glasses and never suffered any loss of vision. When he was over eighty years old, he was found studying by the light of the moon shining in through his window.

The *shammash* of Yeshivas Ohel Moshe was about to climb up on a table one time to take down the plaque of donors whose names they wished to mention in a prayer. The writing was so small that he had to remove the entire plaque in order to read them. But before he could do so, R' Yehoshua Leib, from his place at the eastern wall, began reeling off the names on the plaque hanging on the opposite wall.

CHAPTER TEN

His Personal Practices

1.

He was in the habit of drawing the letters of *Hashem's* Name in the air with his finger, to fulfill his obligation of keeping *Hashem* before one at all times (see *Psalms* 16:8). Even while speaking to people or walking along the street, he would wave his finger back and forth. On *Shabbos* and *Yom Tov*, his fingers rested, but his lips took over, as he murmured the verse over and over.

2.

From the age of thirteen, he never slept in a bed, but would sit at his study until sleep overtook him and he dozed off at his place. He never slept more than two hours at a time, and never wore nightclothes.

3.

He prayed with great concentration and physical effort, sequestered in his room, which no one was ever permitted to enter before noon. His voice could be heard outside. He timed his prayer to coincide with that of the synagogue next to his home, where he went for the reading of the Torah and the priestly blessing.

4.

When he reached the blessing after the *haftarah*, "On His throne no alien shall sit," a torrent of tears would spout from his eyes. When he recited the blessing over the Torah, his face would turn a fiery red.

5.

He would pray for the sick people who turned to him with deep compassion, the tears streaming down when he uttered their names. He invested so much energy in his prayers for sick people that he was upset when someone implored him to pray for a sick person but did not return to tell him when the patient had recovered.

6.

Before praying for a sick person, he would first utter the words, "To You, *Hashem*, is the glory ..." until the words "and to fortify everything" (*I Chronicles* 29:11-12). Then he would commence.

7.

R' Yehoshua Leib owned very few *sefarim*.

8.

No one ever saw him sitting down to a full meal in Jerusalem.

9.

R' Moshe Jules, a Jerusalem pharmacist, won R' Yehoshua Leib's deep respect and affection. R' Yehoshua Leib suffered from a hernia which caused his intestines to become entangled and bulge out, inflicting excruciating pain. R' Moshe was always called to treat him for these attacks. Once, after R' Moshe had reinserted a protruding section, R' Yehoshua Leib begged him to remain close by a little longer, for he feared another such attack. Some time later, it came on and he asked R' Moshe to attend to it again. R' Moshe noticed R' Yehoshua Leib clenching his hands to his heart. He, apparently, was afraid that in his intense pain, he might lower his hands below his waist, something he never did.

10.

He never stood or sat without being fully clothed in a hat and long coat.

11.

He put on special shoes and clothing whenever he had to relieve himself.

12.

He wore a special *gartel* belt directly on his body, in keeping with the opinion of the *Yereim*.

13.

He recited *tikkun chatzos* every midnight. R' Zorach Braverman, who lived in the same courtyard, related how he would hear a bitter wailing in the wee hours of the night, accompanied by a flailing sound coming from his apartment.

14.

Every *erev Rosh Chodesh* he would go to a place near the Temple Mount, which also offered a view of the desolate site of the *Beis Hamikdash*. He would stand there, gaze and weep, and then return home.

15.

R' Yehoshua Leib could often be found standing in his room, peering out the window which faced the Temple Mount, absorbed in thought.

16.

When putting on his *tefillin shel rosh*, he would lower his head all the way to table level, remove the *tefillin* from their small sack and put them right on his head. When he raised his head again, it would be crowned with the *tefillin*.

17.

Someone once bent over towards him while he was reciting the closing paragraph of his *Shemoneh Esrei* and heard him repeating several times, "And all those who rise up and scheme evil against me, speedily confound their counsel and foil their thoughts."

18.

Whenever he came to the eulogy of a scholar, he would stand on his feet throughout the address, his eyes tightly shut.

19.

Whenever he faced a difficult passage in his study, he would say *vidui*, insert a few coins into his charity box and raise his eyes heavenward in prayer: "Favor me, *Hashem*. Enlighten my eyes in Your Torah."

20.

It is said that he never left money in his possession from one week to another. Anything left over was distributed to charity.

21.

He lived in poverty while in Jerusalem, but never accepted money from the community chest. Nor did he accept money from individuals. (He did have a small stipend from the towns where he had served.) He lived a life of unusual privation and denial.

22.

Towards the end of his life, he never ate more than a *kezayis* of bread and only at the *Shabbos* meals.

23.

He followed the example of the Gaon of Vilna in everything he did, and always acted discreetly and modestly.

24.

He often visited the Tomb of the Patriarchs in Chevron and the Cave of Shimon HaTzaddik in Jerusalem.

25.

He was especially cautious about drinking liquids that had been left uncovered, even for a short while. Once, when R' Yehoshua Leib learned that the water which had been used to bake bread had stood uncovered all night long, he refused to touch the bread.

26.

In his household, they made it a practice to put fresh meat into scalding water right after it had been salted and rinsed (following the opinion of *Rambam*).

27.

R' Yehoshua Leib ordered his wife to always follow the stringent ruling, even if this was a minority opinion in the *Shulchan Aruch*.

28.

The salting of meat took precisely one hour, not more or less.

29.

In his household, they used large quantities of salt in *kashering* meat. Once, someone commented to the *rebbetzin* that she had oversalted the meat. R' Yehoshua Leib leaped up to examine the meat and said to his wife, "It is not enough. Salt it some more."

30.

He was careful to keep his vision sanctified. As a rav in Europe, he was approached every *erev Yom Kippur* by women who had discovered questions in the freshly slaughtered chickens. R' Yehoshua Leib would bow his head and fix his gaze upon the ground while the *shammash* brought him each fowl. He would rule on the chicken, face still turned to the ground and not raise his head until all the women had left the house.

31.

R' Yehoshua Leib was careful that from the time a chicken was slaughtered until it was eaten, it should be constantly watched. He also made sure that a Torah scholar supervise the *shochet* while the fowl for his table were being slaughtered.

32.

Before he even stepped foot in Jerusalem, while still in Jaffa, he asked for the traditional Jerusalemite gold-striped caftan. Thus, he entered the holy city in this garb and never wore any other type.

33.

R' Yehoshua Leib never made light of any custom. Asked once to officiate at a wedding, he left when he realized that they were not singing the customary *Mi Adir* under the *chupah*.

34.

It often happened that when a group of people came to receive his blessing, he would bless some and ask the rest to return later.

35.

He made sure to stamp his feet on the floor before entering his house, so as not to frighten those inside with his sudden appearance.

36.

He was vehemently opposed to musical instruments at weddings. In his view, the destruction of the *Beis Hamikdash* is constantly before the eyes of Jerusalemites and they must always be in mourning.

37.

During the time that he stayed in a room on the premises of the Diskin Orphanage, which he founded, he made a point of paying full rent to the orphanage.

38.

He always used the words of *Chazal* in his speech. His disciples said that he never said a sentence for which the parallel could not be found in the phrases of our Sages. Even when addressing people, he would use the language of *Chazal*.

39.

Every *motzaei Shabbos* he would study the weekly portion with his disciples. The clever insights, which he expressed once, were never uttered again, while the simple thoughts repeated themselves year in and year out.

40.

He forbade putting in writing any lenient ruling which he had issued to a particular person and which might be predicated on his particular circumstances.

41.

He was particular that the *sefarim* in his house be properly bound. When *Chiddushei R' Akiva Eiger* first appeared, one of his disciples hastened to bring him a copy, fresh off the press, yet unbound. Despite his thirst to peruse it, he ordered that it first be covered properly and then brought to him.

42.

He took care not to attend a *bris* where *metzitzah* was not properly observed. As for those who were circumcised without *metzitzah*, he wrote, "May Eliyahu come speedily to find a *heter* for those who were thus circumcised so that they might be permitted to eat of the *Pesach* sacrifice."

43.

His *tzitzis* fringes were knotted as follows: first ten, then five, then six, then five, to correspond with the Name of *Hashem*.

44.

He was most reluctant to give his approbation for any *sefer* or to sign any letter of recommendation. Even organizations or institutions which he himself headed did not receive any certification from him. No more than ten such letters or certificates in his hand were ever issued, excluding letters reinforcing the *cherem* against secular schools, which he signed liberally.

45.

His personal seal had the Western Wall and the Tomb of Rachel engraved upon it.

46.

He had an elaborate order of the blowing of the *shofar* on *Rosh Hashanah*, complete with stringencies and exacting measures.

47.

R' Yehoshua Leib was not content with the *tekiyos* he had heard in the synagogue, for fear that not all had been perfect. And so he would listen to the sound of the *shofar* until sunset. The residents of the Old City became accustomed to the *shofar* piercing the air from after the meal until sunset.

48.

His *Yom Kippur Shemoneh Esrei* took such a long time that he usually had time for little more than the four *Shemoneh Esreis*.

49.

On his way back from the *Kosel* one *Chol Hamoed Succos*, he paused to gaze upon the Temple Mount. People saw him stop and, thinking that he was too tired to return to his home in the Kerem neighborhood in the New Quarter, wished to order a wagon to take him home. R' Yehoshua Leib would not hear of it, explaining that he would not sit, even for a short time, outside the *succah*. He began walking in long strides and was soon home.

50.

His greetings to visitors on the Festival was concise. On *Succos*, he would say, "May we be fortunate to sit in the *succah* of Leviathan's skin"; on *Pesach*, "May we partake of the offerings and the *Pesach* sacrifices"; and on *Shavuos*, "May we be fortunate to show our faces in the courtyard [of the *Beis Hamikdash*]."

51.

Once, people noticed a transaction between R' Yehoshua Leib and the *chassan* whose wedding was soon to take place in his courtyard. The young man paid R' Yehoshua Leib a few pennies rent for the four cubits upon which the *chupah* was erected so that it could be considered his property during the ceremony.

52.

On *Purim*, he would drink until he was inebriated, as our Sages prescribed. In one of his letters he writes, "Your letter arrived on *Purim* together with your *chiddushim* in Torah. But since I was preoccupied fulfilling the *mitzvah*, 'A man is obligated to get drunk on *Purim*,' I was unable to concentrate upon it. Now that *Purim* is over, I am able to study what you wrote."

53.

On *Hoshana Rabbah*, R' Yehoshua Leib would beat the willow branches upon the ground with all his might.

54.

On *erev Yom Kippur*, he would nibble on raisins all day long, in keeping with the Sages' teaching that it was a *mitzvah* to eat.

55.

He had a new table made for himself every *Pesach*.

56.

He ate *matzah* only on the first night of *Pesach*.

57.

He had a special kitchen which was used only for *Pesach*.

58.

On *Pesach*, they used only glass dishes in his household and cooked in iron pots.

59.

Someone once brought him a new fruit from India. He first put on his festival clothing and then recited the *shehecheyanu* blessing.

60.

While living in Jerusalem, he put on his *Yom Tov* clothing when he went to greet R' Shneur Zalman from Lublin.

61.

R' Yehoshua Leib maintained that it was forbidden to insert one's hand into the cracks of the *Kosel* (due to its holiness).

CHAPTER ELEVEN

Peer Opinion of R' Yehoshua Leib

he Malbim was once enumerating the praises of the rabbis of his generation. Someone asked him why he had omitted mention of R' Yehoshua Leib. He replied, "I am an expert at evaluating gold and silver, but I have no knowledge of precious gems."

R' Yosef Dov Ber Soloveitchik used the title of "Rebbe" or *"mashiach Hashem"* when he referred to R' Yehoshua Leib, without even mentioning his name. He took it for granted that people knew whom he was referring to.

He once said to the author of *Tzir Ne'eman*, "I have wanted to write a letter to our teacher in Jerusalem, but each time I lift my pen, my hand begins quaking violently."

The author of *Chevel Yaakov*, disciple of R' Yehoshua Leib, often visited R' Yosef Dov Ber Soloveitchik and told over his master's *chiddushim*. That great man would pace the length of his room and drink in R' Yehoshua Leib's words thirstily, murmuring all the while, "What profound concepts!"

R' Yosef Dov Ber was once in excellent spirits. He beamed brightly. When they asked him why, he replied, "I received a letter from R' Yehoshua Leib today, and I feel like it is a *Yom Tov*."

R' Yechiel Heller, author of *Amudei Or*, served in Suwalk while R' Yehoshua Leib served in Lomza. R' Yehoshua Leib's disciples often visited him and reviewed the *chiddushim* they had heard from their master. And he would exclaim, "Then the likes of the *Hafla'ah* lives in our generation! I must go and listen in on his lessons!"

The *Chiddushei HaRim*, the Gerrer Rebbe, greatly revered R' Yehoshua Leib. Whenever *chassidim* from Lomza came to him, he would inquire about R' Yehoshua Leib and send back his warm regards. They had met once at the home of R' Dov Berish Meislish in Warsaw and the Gerrer Rebbe was deeply impressed by R' Yehoshua Leib's grandeur.

R' Yitzchak Elchanan Spector was a childhood friend of R' Yehoshua Leib and had studied together with him under his father, R' Binyamin Diskin. He would utter R' Yehoshua Leib's name with veneration and referred to him in writing as "the pride and glory of our times."

R' Chaim Soloveitchik used to say, "At that point where the titles and praises of all the *gedolim* of our times ends, titles such as *rav*, *gaon*, *gaon gadol*, *rosh kol bnei hagolah* and others — that is where his tributes begin." He spoke of him as "Holy unto Hashem." R' Chaim described R' Yehoshua Leib as "unique in his generation in not leaving a successor of his stature" and "unmatched even in many of the generations preceding him,"

A Jerusalem *esrog* dealer, R' Naftali, son of the author of *Maskil LeEisan*, went abroad and spent some time in Brisk. He went to R' Chaim and begged him to intercede with R' Yehoshua Leib in Jerusalem concerning *esrogim* from Corfu. R' Chaim sat down to write a letter, but drew back, saying that his conscience would not allow him to address himself to R' Yehoshua Leib, especially when he recalled how his saintly father, R' Yosef Dov Ber, would tremble at the mere mention of his name.

R' Chaim once said, "Had R' Yehoshua Leib lived in the times of the Rama, he would also have been considered a *gaon*."

A heavy snow mixed with hail once fell in Horodna and piled up on roofs and houses. The city was blanketed with a thick covering of snow and ice. The streets were deserted; there was no sign of a living thing. But, at dawn, whom should people see from their windows but R' Nachum, shivering with cold, sweeping the snow drifts to the right and left and blazing a path down the street.

He later explained, "R' Yehoshua Leib must pass here. I am clearing a path for him so that he will not have to walk in the snow."

R' Elya Chaim Meisel of Lodz used to bake *Pesach matzos* with his own hands to bring to R' Yehoshua Leib in Lomza. He would say, "I would run by foot eighty miles to please him."

R' Yosef Rosen, the Rogatchover Gaon, described his rebbe as another R' Akiva Eiger, a judgment shared by R' Yehoshua Leib's great colleague in Jerusalem, R' Shmuel Salant.

R' Elazar Mendel Biderman once came with a group of his *chassidim* to pray at the cave of Shimon HaTzaddik. There he saw R' Yehoshua Leib inside by himself and refused to enter, even though the *chassidim* strongly urged him to do so. He stood outside with his retinue and waited silently for a long time before the door to the tomb opened and R' Yehoshua Leib emerged.

R' Yitzchak Yerucham Diskin, R' Yehoshua Leib's only son, had to summon all his courage before sitting down to write a letter to his holy father.

Once, when R' Yitzchak Yerucham was already fifty-four years old, he wrote a letter filled with his *chiddushim* to his father. When his father failed to respond, he wrote a broken-hearted letter: "My soul pines for your holy answer and I long to know why it was not forthcoming; if there is a reason, it is something I must know and learn from. For if you do not criticize or praise my innovations, why must I continue to toil so hard? And so, I decided to try again in the hope that I would receive instruction from your holy mouth."

R' Yosef Chaim Sonnenfeld, chief rabbi of Jerusalem, was told that R' Yehoshua Leib descended from the House of David. He commented, "Anyone with eyes in his head can see from his features that this is so."

After R' Yehoshua Leib's death, R' Yosef Chaim Sonnenfeld often visited his grave and recited the entire *Tehillim* there. He did not miss any of R' Yehoshua Leib's *yahrzeits*. Even in 5691 (1931), when he was eighty-three, he climbed up to the grave on a wet and stormy day. The wind was so strong that it blew him to the ground and he scraped his face.

R' Shimon Menashe, rabbi of Hebron, was blind at the end of his days. Whenever R' Yehoshua Leib visited Hebron, he would say, "Would that *Hashem* opened up my eyes for a short while so that I could merit gazing upon the radiance of R' Yehoshua Leib's face."

R' Chaim Berlin, son of the *Netziv*, wrote of R' Yehoshua Leib, "It is superfluous to heap words [of praise] upon the master of Israel, the brilliant and saintly rabbi of Brisk. It is like attesting to the brilliance of the sun at noontime."

R' Yaakov Orenstein from Jerusalem was R' Yehoshua Leib's devoted disciple from the time of his arrival until his death. Once, R' Yaakov was sitting among his disciples, lavishing praise upon one of the great men of his generation. He described how he had written his monumental work, which was hailed by all his peers. He never had time to prepare his writings for the printer because he was so preoccupied with his rabbinical duties. Whenever the printer came to ask him for some more material, and he had nothing ready to give him, he would ask the printer to wait while he sat down to produce a page or two without resorting to any references or sources.

R' Yaakov became so worked up over his description that one of his disciples asked if that scholar could be compared to the Brisker Rav. R' Yaakov was stunned. "What?!" he cried out. "The Brisker Rav? He is an angel. Who can begin to fathom his greatness? Who can begin to understand him? He is awesome, awesome, far removed from his generation."

CHAPTER TWELVE

The Soul Departs

TUESDAY, THE TWENTY-FOURTH of *Teves*, 5658 (1898).
R' Yehoshua Leib's health had been poor for the previous two
Last Days weeks. His doctors hovered about his bed, doing
their utmost, but he was becoming weaker by the
hour. On Tuesday morning, his condition deteriorated. Pneumonia
was beginning to take its toll. The team of doctors shook their heads
gravely towards the disciples swarming outside, indicating that the
situation was hopeless.

R' Yehoshua Leib felt that his hours were numbered. He called to
the *rebbetzin* and asked for some water to wash his hands and a small
measure of bread, to gain the *mitzvah* of *birkas hamazon* for the last
time on earth. She fetched these at once.

Men, women and children streamed to the synagogues and the
yeshivos to pray for mercy. The huge Beis Yaakov synagogue was
filled to capacity with people who dropped everything and came to
beseech their Creator not to extinguish His light. The prayers
continued for four consecutive days and the sound of the *shofaros*,
prayers and *Selichos* shook and reverberated throughout the city.

R' Yehoshua Leib's disciples dispatched cables to all Jewish cities abroad, begging people to pray for his recovery.

A serious turn for the worse took place on Thursday night. R' Shmuel Salant ordered criers to circulate throughout the Old City and the neighborhoods in the New City announcing that everyone was required, by summons of the rabbis, to rise at dawn and gather in the houses of worship for prayer: men, women and children.

That night was an anxious one for everyone. Shortly after the fearful announcement, the synagogues were filled to bursting. The *aron kodesh* was opened for the recital of *Tehillim, Selichos, Hoshanos* and the *yud-gimmel midos* accompanied by the blowing of *shofaros*. Little *cheder* children were seated separately with their teachers; their heartfelt wailing soared above the sound of the other worshipers.

In R' Shmuel Salant's synagogue, the spiritual arousal reached its peak. It was an awesome, heartbreaking sight. The elders and scholars of Jerusalem sobbed openly. The groaning of the elderly and the wailing of the young *yeshivah* children reached a crescendo through the stillness of night and became one powerful cry. Tears mingled with tears. The venerable rav of Jerusalem stood upon his feet, mustering the remnant of his strength. His head was bent, his face turned to the eastern wall. He wept silently in front of the open ark, his lips moving and the tears flowing thickly from blinded eyes.

A large portion of Jerusalem Jewry fasted that day, as did the orphans of the Diskin Home. Young children ceased their study in order to pray and arouse Heavenly mercy. Slowly, stores and workshops shut down and multitudes swept towards the tombs of *tzaddikim*, whether to the *Me'aras Hamachpelah* in Hebron or the Tomb of Rachel in Beis Lechem, to the graves on Mount Olives or the Cave of Shimon HaTzaddik.

In all the cities throughout the land, people gathered at public prayer rallies. In Jaffa, R' Naftali Hertz summoned the entire city to an assembly for prayer.

In these final three days, R' Yehoshua Leib remained enveloped in his *tallis* and crowned in his *tefillin*, deeply contemplative. He appeared like a holy angel. Only his lips moved. His pure eyes burned like torches and his whole being radiated an awesome grandeur.

Before the approach of *Shabbos*, R' Yehoshua Leib removed his *tefillin* and held them tenderly in both palms, kissing them fervently. He laid them down, but picked them up again, reluctant to part with them. He must have realized that this would be a final parting.

The *shofar* announcing the arrival of the *Shabbos* could be heard outside. His lips were sealed as far as others were concerned. He remained motionless. Only his pure eyes remained open, beaming forth majestic radiance.

The candles were lit. R' Yehoshua Leib's crystal-clear eyes burned like those flames. Several of his closest disciples sat in an inner room, eating the meal and softly singing the *zemiros*, careful not to disturb their master; they were resolved to spend their *Shabbos* within his four cubits.

That *Shabbos* was very different from any other. Jerusalemites could not remember another one so fraught with emotion and tension. Throughout the day, his disciples walked the streets, calling for reinforcements for prayers for the master's recovery. Announcements were made from hour to hour until evening.

As dusk was descending, during that special time of Heavenly grace called *raava d'raavin*, masses streamed towards R' Yehoshua Leib's *beis medrash* for the evening prayer. Most of the synagogues in the city emptied out and the compressed crowd filled the hall of Yeshivas Ohel Moshe and the immense courtyard outside. The steps outside were also packed with people.

Twilight descended. The disciples in his room shut the door in face of the constant flow of people pushing their way in to pray as close as possible to their beloved master.

Shabbos was over. Someone recited *havdalah*. As soon as it was over, R' Yehoshua Leib breathed his last in purity, surrounded by his disciples, who cried out, *"Shema Yisrael . . ."*

THE ENORMOUS CROWD OUTSIDE heard the thunderous cry and burst through the doors to add their voices.

Jerusalem Mourns

News of the tragedy spread rapidly throughout the city. Jerusalem sank into deep mourning. Overcome with grief, Jerusalemites shut themselves in their homes and bemoaned their great loss in the words of

Lamentations recited on a *motzaei Shabbos*, "All pleasantness ceased on that *motzaei Shabbos*."

R' Shmuel Salant and his *beis din* called an emergency meeting to discuss the funeral arrangements. He expressed his fear of holding it that same night. The winding lanes through which the procession would have to pass were narrow and the night dark with a thick mist. It was more than likely that people would be trampled. Besides, all of Jerusalem would attend such a historic event. The city would empty out and thieves would have a heyday. No, it was altogether too risky, said R' Shmuel. He advised postponing the funeral until the next day, even though, customarily, one did not leave the dead in Jerusalem overnight.

The rabbis issued a joint proclamation, announced by criers throughout the city streets, that the funeral would take place on Sunday.

But a sizable portion of the Jerusalem population could not wait and began streaming towards R' Yehoshua Leib's house. The pure body was surrounded by the prominent scholars of Jerusalem and his foremost disciples. R' Yosef Chaim Sonnenfeld, R' Yaakov Orenstein and other disciples wept bitterly until dawn.

With morning, it was announced that anyone whose sons or daughters were enrolled in the secular schools was not to touch the bier. Those who were to bear it were required to immerse themselves in a *mikveh* beforehand.

R' Shmuel Salant, the *Rishon LeZion* R' Yaakov Shaul Elyashar, and the *batei din* of both Ashkenazic and Sephardic communities called for all workshops and stores to close for the entire day. The *yeshivos* and *chadarim* were similarly closed.

After the morning prayers, thousands of Jerusalemites swept towards the street in front of R' Yehoshua Leib's house. Their numbers swelled from one moment to the next. The entire city emptied out, including the neighborhoods outside the wall. Traffic stopped. There was not a soul to be seen. The police had to send mounted troops to guard the deserted property throughout the city. All the squares and streets leading towards R' Yehoshua Leib's house were filled with a sea of people. Roofs and porches were packed tightly with weeping people from all the segments of the population.

After the body was purified, it was removed from the house and taken to the *beis medrash* where R' Yosef Chaim Sonnenfeld eulogized his master. Then R' Yaakov Shaul Elyashar offered his eulogy. He was followed by R" Avraham Abba, the noted *av beis din* and others.

The bier was carried by the most venerable of Jerusalem's great men. It passed through the city streets and turned towards the Rabbi Yehudah Hechassid Synagogue in the Jewish market square. There, R' Shmuel Salant and R' Shneur Zalman of Lublin awaited it.

The children of the Diskin Orphanage, doubly orphaned now that their mentor was gone, went before the bier and were followed by rows upon rows of boys from all the *chadarim* in the city, Ashkenazim and Sephardim alike.

It was difficult work wending one's way through the thousands of compressed people packed all the way from R' Yehoshua Leib's house until the Churvah synagogue. It took all morning for the procession to finally reach the courtyard.

The synagogue, the large courtyard, rooms, balconies and stairs in the vicinity were black with frocked figures pressing against one another. After another difficult struggle, the stretcher was carried into the synagogue, which was ablaze with light. Jerusalem's two most venerated figures, R' Shmuel Salant and R' Shneur Zalman of Lublin, sat bowed on the high central *bimah*. A large table had been set before it to bear R' Yehoshua Leib's stretcher.

The congestion increased. The gates had to be locked to prevent yet more from pushing their way in.

The elderly R' Shmuel Salant rose and the wailing increased. He began in a tear-choked voice with the verse, "The joy of our heart has ceased, our dance had been turned to mourning ..." His address was interrupted from time to time by the keening of the assembled or when the venerable sage himself, tears streaming down unto the bier, was overcome with emotion.

He was followed by a brief eulogy from the *Gaon* of Lublin which was cut short due to his weakness. He quickly concluded with a heartfelt, tear-ridden *kaddish*. Several people fainted. The doors were opened and the stretcher was carried out and towards Mount Olives.

The funeral proceeded until the large square before the Zion Gate. In this open space, one could first begin to appreciate the size of the gathering. It was an awesome sight, reaching from that large square all the way to the slopes of the mountain.

R' Yitzchak Winograd, *Rosh Yeshivah* of Toras Chaim, spoke. His thunderous voice highlighted the battle which R' Yehoshua Leib had waged for the purity of Torah education and all that he had sacrificed for it. And he concluded, quoting, "Who shall stand up against the doers of evil?"

The procession paused upon reaching Yad Avshalom and more eulogies were offered, first by the Rav of Plonsk and then by others. The funeral procession continued up the slopes of Mount Olives which overlook the Temple Mount. That is where they dug his grave and laid him to rest.

Tomb of
R' Yehoshua
Leib Diskin
on the
Mount of Olives

Crushed by their loss, the mourners shuffled their way back to the city without their beloved rabbi. And the Holy City was shrouded in gloom over its misfortune. The guardian of its walls would guard no more.

The news of R' Yehoshua Leib's death created shock waves throughout the Diaspora. Communities all over the world sank into mourning. They held eulogies which were addressed by the most distinguished scholars of each place.

Jerusalem was bereft of its guide, its shield, its protective shade. Israel was without its chariot and horseman.

✑ Glossary

Glossary

All Entries are Hebrew unless otherwise indicated.

Adar — the twelfth month (beginning from Nissan) of the Jewish year in which *Purim* is celebrated.

agunah (pl. *agunos*) — woman whose marital status is uncertain because she has neither a divorce nor evidence of her missing husband's death.

aleph-beis — the Hebrew alphabet.

Amen — the word recited after hearing a blessing; so be it.

apikores — freethinker, heretic, agnostic.

apikorsus — heresy, atheism, skepticism.

Ari Hakadosh — Rabbi Yitzchak Luria, the fountainhead of modern Kabbalistic thought.

aron kodesh — ark in which Torah scrolls are kept.

Ashkenazic — Jewry of North, West and Central Europe or their customs.

askan (pl. *askanim*) — communal worker.

Av — the fifth month (beginning from Nissan) of the Jewish year in which both Temples were destroyed.

av beis din — chief judge of a rabbinical court of law.

bachur'l — *bochur* (diminutive) — young unmarried man.

bar mitzvah — religious coming of age on a boy's thirteenth birthday.

beis din (pl. *batei din*) — rabbinic court for deciding matters of Torah law.

beis Midrash (pl. *batei medrash*) — study hall.

Bava Metzia — a tractate of the Talmud, middle section of the order *Nezikin* in the Mishnah.

Beis Hamikdash — Holy Temple in Jerusalem.

ben yeshivah — one who studies in a yeshivah.

Berachos — A tractate of the Talmud.

bimah — podium from which the Torah is read in synagogue; also used for communal announcements after the synagogue service.

birkas hamazon — Grace after Meals.

bris — circumcision.

Chacham Bashi — Sephardic Chief Rabbi; Chacham Bashi of Jerusalem was also known as Rishon leZion.

cheder (pl. *chadorim*) — elementary school for religious studies.

chametz — leavening; the substance required to be removed from one's possession before Passover.

chassan (pl. *chasanim*) — bridegroom.

Chassid (pl. *chassidim*) — adherent of Chassidism — a pietist movement founded by Reb Yisrael Baal Shem Tov in the 18th century.

Chazal — (abbreviation for Chachameinu, Zichronom Livrachah) our Sages, of blessed memory, specifically the Rabbis of the Talmud.

chazzan — person who leads a prayer service, cantor.

cherem — excommunication, ban.

chessed — kindness.

chevra kadisha — burial society.

Chevras Mishnayos — a group organized for studying of Mishnah.

Chevras Shas — a group organized for study of Talmud.

chiddush (pl. *chiddushim*) — Torah novellae; original analyses and interpretations of difficult points of Torah.

Chol Hamoed Succos — intermediate days of Succos.

chupah — (a) the wedding canopy; (b) the ceremony constituting the legal completion of the marriage.

daf — a *blatt* — one full leaf (two pages) of the Talmud.

dayan (pl. *dayanim*) — rabbinic court judge.

Days of Judgment — *Rosh Hashanah* and *Yom Kippur.*

din Torah — (lit. "judgment of Torah") — an adversary proceeding before a court of Jewish law.

Elul — the sixth month (from Nissan).

Eretz Yisrael — Land of Israel.

erev Yom Kippur — *Yom Kippur* eve.

eruv (*chatzeiros* — courtyards) — a legal device which merges several separate ownerships (*reshus hayachid*) into a single joint ownership. Each resident family of a *chatzeir* contributes food to the *eruv* which is then placed in one of the dwellings of the *chatzeir*. This procedure allows us to view all the houses opening into the courtyard as the property of a single consortium (composed of all residents of the courtyard) thereby permitting all participating residents to carry items on the Sabbath from the houses into the *chatzeir* and from one house to another.

esrog (pl. *esrogim*) — the citron fruit, one of the Four Species used in the festivities on Succos.

gabbai (pl. *gabbaim*) — (a) synagogue official; (b) overseer of charity funds; (c) shamash.

gadol — Torah leader.

Gan Eden — Garden of Eden.

gaon — genius; brilliant Torah scholar.

gaon gadol — a great genius.

gedolim — Torah leaders of the generation.

gehinnom — hell.

Gemara — that portion of the Talmud which discusses the Mishnah; also, loosely, a synonym for the Talmud as a whole.

Gevald — help!

hachnosas orchim — hospitality.

haftarah — a portion of the Prophets read at the completion of the public Torah reading on *Shabbos* and festivals.

halachic — accepted ruling in cases of disagreement based on Jewish law.

Hashem — (lit. "the Name"); a way of referring to God without pronouncing the Sacred Name.

Haskalah — (so-called) Enlightenment Movement which disregarded many Torah traditions.

havdalah — ceremony concluding the Sabbath.

heter (pl. *heterim*) — permit, license.

hiddur (pl. *hiddurim*) — enhancement or meticulous observance of a *mitzvah* beyond the basic requirements.

Hoshanah Rabbah — the seventh day of the *Succos* Festival, when seven circuits are made around the *bimah* in synagogue.

Iyar — the second month (from Nissan) in which *Lag BaOmer* is celebrated.

kaddish — (lit. "holy"); passage with congregational responses recited by *chazzan* or a mourner.

kavanah (pl. *kavanos*) — intent, concentration.

kesubah — the marriage contract which a man must give to his bride guaranteeing her financial security and other martial rights.

Kesubos — a tractate of the Talmud.

kezayis — the volume of an olive or half an egg (somewhat more than the volume of one fluid ounce).

Kislev — ninth month (from Nissan) of the Jewish calendar, *Chanukah* is celebrated beginning on the 25th of Kislev.

Kol Nidre — inaugural prayer which begins the *Yom Kippur* service.

Kollel (pl. *kollelim*) — the institutions in *Eretz Yisrael* founded by European Jewry to help settle *Eretz Yisrael*, funded from abroad which supported many of Jerusalem's residents; usually organized along national lines, with people being supported by the national organization of their country of origin.

kosel — Western (Wailing) Wall.

kosher — ritually fit for use.

Maariv — evening prayers.

maggid — preacher; especially, the officially recognized preacher of a city.
malach — angel.

Mashiach — the Messiah.

maskil (pl. *maskilim*) — follower of *Haskalah*.

mazel tov — (lit. "good luck"); congratulations.

melamed — teacher, especially of young children.

melave malka — meal eaten after *Havdalah* in honor of the departing Sabbath.

meshumad — apostate.

metzitzah — sucking out (ritually, of circumcision blood).

mezuzah — tiny parchment scroll affixed to doorpost, containing the first two paragraphs of *Shema Yisrael*.

Midah K'Neged Midah — measure for measure, retaliation.

middos — character traits.

Minchah — afternoon prayers.

minyan — quorum of ten men for conducting a prayer service.

mishnah — the teachings of the Tannaim which form the basis of the Talmud. (Its final form was established by Rabbi Yehudah HaNasi).

mitzvah (pl. *mitzvos*) — Torah commandment.

motzaei Shabbos — time of departure of the Sabbath.

nachas — pleasure.

Nezikin — the fourth division of the Mishnah.

Nissan — the first month, it is when Passover is celebrated.

olam hazeh — (lit. "this world"); refers to the pleasures of this world or in general life on earth.

Perushim — community founded by the disciples of the Vilna Gaon and subsequently joined by many pious non-Lithuanian immigrants.

Pesach — Passover, one of the three Pilgrim festivals, beginning on the 15th of Nissan.

pilpul — fine-honed halachic debate.

posek — those who rule on disputed halachic issues, arbiter.

poskim — rabbinic authority on *halachic* questions; literature on such questions.

Purim — Holiday celebrating the rescue of the Jews in Persia from the decree of the wicked Haman as recorded in the Book of *Esther*, read twice on the holiday — 14 Adar.

rabbanus — rabbinate.

Rashi — R' Shlomo ben Yitzchak; most famous and most widely studied commentator on Scripture and Talmud (France 1040-1105).

rav — rabbi.

rebbetzin — rabbi's wife.

Rishon leZion — Sephardic Chief Rabbi.

rosh chodesh Menachem Av — first day of the month of Av.

Rosh Hashanah — Jewish New Year.

rosh kol bnei hagolah — the leader of Diaspora Jewry.

rosh mesivta — dean of a mesivta — yeshivah high school.

Rosh Yeshivah (pl. *roshei yeshivah*) — dean of a yeshivah.

Sabbath Bride — the Sabbath personified as a bride or queen.

sandak — one who holds the baby while the circumcision is being performed.

Sanhedrin — (a) Supreme Rabbinic Court in the times of the Holy Temple comprised of 71 judges. (b) A tractate of the Talmud.

Sefardic — (lit. from Sefarad — Spain); Middle Eastern Jews or their customs.

sefarim — books, especially on Torah subjects.

segulah — spiritual remedy; talisman.

Selichos — penitential prayers; specifically those recited on fast days and during the period preceding and following Rosh Hashanah.

shaatnez — mixture of linen and wool which is forbidden to be worn by a Jewish person.

Shabbos — the Sabbath.

shammash — (a) synagogue caretaker; (b) rabbi's assistant or personal secretary.

Shavuos — the festival commemorating the receiving of the Torah at Sinai.

Shechinah — Divine Presence.

shechitah — ritual slaughter.

shehechiyanu — blessing of thanksgiving recited upon (a) eating seasonal fruits of a new season for the first time; (b) purchasing a new garment of significant value to the wearer; (c) performance of a seasonal mitzvah; or (d) deriving significant benefit from an event.

Shema Yisrael — prayer recited twice each day, it begins *Shema Yisrael* — "Hear O Israel, Hashem is our God, Hashem is One."

Shemittah — the Sabbatical year, during which the Torah commands that land in *Eretz Yisrael* be left fallow.

Shemoneh Esrei — the *amidah* section of the daily prayer; the "Eighteen Blessings."

Shir Hamaalos — Psalm 126 recited before Grace after Meals on Sabbath, Festivals and joyous events.

shiur (pl. *shiurim*) — lesson, especially a Torah lesson.

shochet — ritual slaughterer.

shul (Yiddish) — synagogue.

Shulchan — table on the *bimah* used for Torah reading and by *chazzan* from where he conducts the prayer services.

Shulchan Aruch — Code of Jewish Law.

sofer — scribe.

succah —a booth in which the Jewish is commanded to dwell during the festival of *Succos*.

Succos — Tabernacles.

tallis — large, fringed shawl, usually worn draped over one's outer garments while praying.

talmid chacham — Torah scholar.

talmidim — students, disciples.

Talmud Bavli — the Babylonian Talmud.

Talmud Yerushalmi — the Jerusalem Talmud completed in *Eretz Yisrael* at the end of the fourth century C.E.

tefillin — phylacteries.

tefillin shel rosh — phylacteries worn on the head.

Tehillim — the Book of *Psalms*.

tekiyos — one of the sounds of the shofar.

Ten Days of Repentance — the ten-day period between *Rosh Hashanah* and *Yom Kippur* during which time *teshuvah* (repentance) is uniquely acceptable.

Teves — tenth month (starting from Nissan) of Jewish year.

tikkun— lit. "improvement"; source of merit for the departed soul.

Tikkun Chatzos — a post-midnight service adopted by certain saintly people.

tzaddik (pl. *tzaddikim*) — saintly person.

tzitzis — small fringed garment worn beneath one's outer garments the entire day.

veshinantam levanecha — "And you shall teach your children" (*Deuteronomy* 6:7).

vidui — confession of sins.

yahrzeit — the anniversary of a person's passing.

yehareg ve'al yaavor — "rather give up your life than transgress" — rather than commit any of the three cardinal sins one should choose to give up his life.

Yereim — G-d-fearing.

yeshivah (pl. *yeshivos*) — Talmudic academy.

yishuv — the Jewish settlement in *Eretz Yisrael*; the old *yishuv* was comprised of the original Jewish settlers, generally those coming before the 1880's, an extremely religious group.

Yom Tov — Festival day.

Yoreh De'ah — one of the four parts of the *Shulchan Aruch*.

yud-gimmel midos — the Thirteen Attributes.

zemiros — songs of praise; especially those sung at the *Shabbos* and *Yom Tov* meals.

Zeraim — *Mishnah Seder Zeraim* — one of the six *sedarim* (divisions) of Mishnah.

This volume is part of
THE ARTSCROLL SERIES®
an ongoing project of
translations, commentaries and expositions
on Scripture, Mishnah, Talmud, Halachah,
liturgy, histroy, the classic Rabbinic writings,
biographies, and thought.

For a brochure of current publications
visit your local Hebrew bookseller
or contact the publisher:

Mesorah Publications, ltd

4401 Second Avenue
Brooklyn, New York 11232
(718) 921-9000